Headquarters United States Air Force

Reinvigorating the Air Force Nuclear Enterprise

Prepared by the Air Force Nuclear Task Force
24 October 2008

U.S. AIR FORCE

Integrity - Service - Excellence

Air Force Nuclear Task Force

Director
Major General C. Donald Alston
Director, Nuclear Operations, Plans, & Requirements
DCS/Operations, Plans, & Requirements

Integrity - Service - Excellence

OCT 2 4 2008

MEMORANDUM FOR SECRETARY OF DEFENSE

SUBJECT: The Strategic Plan to Reinvigorate the Air Force Nuclear Enterprise

Reinvigorating the Air Force Nuclear Enterprise is our highest priority. We've taken many actions over the past year based on the recommendations of several internal and external investigations, but more work remains. We have developed a strategic plan to revitalize the nuclear enterprise and reclaim the trust of our nation and confidence of our allies.

The attached document details our strategic plan for achieving this important objective. The plan synthesizes recommendations and findings from several internal and external investigations of Air Force stewardship of nuclear sustainment and operations. It outlines the many complex and interdependent factors that degraded the Air Force nuclear enterprise. Most importantly, it identifies the key principles that will guide the Air Force as it recommits to this critical mission area.

Credible nuclear deterrence is essential to the security of the Nation, our allies and our friends. As outlined in the roadmap, the Air Force intends to fully restore its credibility by improving unity of command and effort, developing the technical skills of Air Force personnel, reinforcing the nuclear mission responsibilities, promoting a culture of compliance and precision and improving enterprise-wide oversight.

The American people depend on the United States Air Force to deliver secure and reliable nuclear deterrence capabilities and have done so for over 61 years. America's Airmen accept this mission with pride, professionalism and a solemn commitment to the highest standards of excellence.

MICHAEL B. DONLEY
Secretary of the Air Force

NORTON A. SCHWARTZ
General, USAF
Chief of Staff

Table of Contents

Executive Summary

Commitment to Change

Reinvigorating the Air Force Nuclear Enterprise is our highest priority. We've taken many actions over the past year based on the recommendations of several internal and external investigations, but more work remains. We have developed a strategic plan to revitalize the nuclear enterprise and reclaim the trust of our nation and confidence of our allies. We need the commitment of every Airman to this priority.

This roadmap identifies a comprehensive set of actions the Air Force must and will take to overcome documented deficiencies and set the conditions for sustainable excellence across the Air Force nuclear enterprise.

Strategic Context

At the end of the Cold War, significant changes in the global security environment prompted Air Force senior leaders to restructure the force. Anticipating and adapting to global challenges, commanders at all levels shaped the combat forces under their control through a number of initiatives. In his 2008 report to the Secretary of Defense, Dr. Schlesinger stated, "Changes made by the Air Force after the Cold War were in response to the defense downsizing of the 1990s as well as national leadership priorities." During that time, "the Air Force and other services were experiencing severe resource constraints. With less national emphasis on nuclear weapons during this period, the Air Force failed to grasp the continued need to maintain a viable airpower-based nuclear deterrent capability. Moreover, as the size of the nuclear arsenal was reduced and emphasis shifted to conventional missions, the Air Force failed to articulate the continuing value of the nuclear deterrent."[1]

The primary cause of the systemic breakdowns in the Air Force's nuclear enterprise was the failure of leadership at many levels to provide proper emphasis on the nuclear mission. The loss of focus stemmed from changes in the operating environment at the end of the Cold War, exacerbated by the profound changes in the security environment following the 9/11 terrorist attacks. In 1992, the Air Force implemented the largest organizational change since its inception leading to the **organizational and supervisory fragmentation of the nuclear enterprise.** This was reinforced by the 1995 Base Realignment and Closure decisions that dispersed depot support for nuclear systems and components. As a result, the Air Force's **nuclear sustainment system became fragmented**, the pool of nuclear experienced Airmen atrophied, and **nuclear expertise eroded** as less time was allocated to maintain nuclear operational proficiency. The Air Force failed to properly resource many nuclear mission areas effectively relegating the Air Force's nuclear enterprise to a 'care-taker' status with limited modernization or recapitalization. The Global War on Terror (GWOT) and

---

[1] Report of the Secretary of Defense Task Force on DoD Nuclear Weapons Management Phase I: The Air Force's Nuclear Mission, September 2008, page 21.

Operations ENDURING FREEDOM (OEF) and IRAQI FREEDOM (OIF) further shifted focus and institutional priorities away from the nuclear mission. Subsequently, Air Force leadership failed to advocate, oversee, and properly emphasize the maintenance of nuclear-related skill sets. **Deficiencies in inspection processes also contributed to the erosion of the culture of accountability and rigorous self-assessment associated with high standards of excellence.**

Recent Events and Recurring Themes

The erosion of mission focus was highlighted by two recent events. In 2006, critical, nuclear-related ICBM parts, labeled as helicopter batteries, were mistakenly sent to Taiwan. In 2007, a B-52 crew mistakenly flew six nuclear weapons from Minot AFB, North Dakota to Barksdale AFB, Louisiana. These incidents triggered a series of reviews and investigations ordered by the Secretary of Defense and the Secretary of the Air Force. The reports converged on six recurring themes reiterated in the Schlesinger Task Force Report:

- Underinvestment in the nuclear deterrence mission is evident, undercutting the nation's deterrence posture – no comprehensive process exists to ensure sustained investment advocacy

- Nuclear-related authority and responsibility are fragmented

- Processes for uncovering, analyzing, and addressing nuclear-related compliance and capability issues are largely ineffective

- Nuclear-related expertise has eroded

- A critical self-assessment culture is lacking

- Air Force Nuclear culture has atrophied resulting in a diminished sense of mission importance, discipline, and excellence

Change Imperative

First, we must address the institutional, long-term commitment to the nuclear deterrence mission. We must re-establish our nuclear culture of discipline and accountability, re-kindle pride in our mission, and renew our heritage of excellence as we reinvigorate the Air Force nuclear enterprise. We face an uncertain and potentially dangerous future that includes nuclear weapons. More countries possess nuclear weapons than during the Cold War, and that number is likely to grow. While we faced many security challenges during the Cold War, over time, we came to understand the motivations and the likely responses of the single adversary that could do catastrophic harm to the United States and our allies. Today, we face national and transnational adversaries whose motivations and responses are perhaps less predictable and have potential to do great harm to the United States or our allies.

First Principles of Rebuilding the Air Force Nuclear Enterprise

Credible strategic deterrence, with unwavering commitment to nuclear deterrence as its cornerstone, is foundational to the security of our nation, allies, and friends. The roadmap, *Reinvigorating the USAF Nuclear Enterprise* is our strategic plan to ensure day-to-day excellence in the stewardship of our nuclear deterrence capability, mission and enterprise. These changes will be institutionalized across our nuclear enterprise ensuring our commitment to excellence regardless of changes to our force structure, competing mission requirements, or the size of our nuclear arsenal. The hallmarks of our performance standards when it comes to the nuclear deterrence mission are precision and reliability. A culture of compliance, clear organizational structures, and active governance processes are the principal pillars to help us achieve sustained excellence in this most vital mission area.

We must build a composite structure of sustainment, operational, and Headquarters Air Force organizations that are appropriately resourced with focused processes to ensure safe, secure, reliable operations. We must enable current and future capability, advocacy, and a culture of compliance; institutional focus; accountability/oversight; and provide governance of these activities--a principal focus of this roadmap.

Extended Deterrence

Credible nuclear deterrence is essential to our security and that of our allies and friends. Many allied and friendly countries continue to depend on the security umbrella provided by the nuclear deterrence capability of the United States. In the absence of this "security umbrella," some non-nuclear allies might perceive a need to develop and deploy their own nuclear capability.[2] **Recent geopolitical events underscore the necessity for extended deterrence.**

The Air Force provides two of the three critical legs of the nation's nuclear deterrent forces. Flexible Air Force bombers and forward-based, dual-capable aircraft (DCA) fighters best exploit the political element of nuclear weapons by being able to visibly demonstrate resolve or the potential for escalation through the scalable generation of forces and recallable airborne alert postures. Ready, capable, and secure ICBMs provide the unique, sovereign-based, stabilizing, and responsive capability to hold any target on the globe at risk 24/7.

Objectives of the Air Force Nuclear Roadmap

The Air Force will not simply chart a path to resolve the six recurring themes/problem areas discussed earlier. The composite actions that comprise this roadmap will reestablish a recognized standard of excellence in the United States Air Force's nuclear enterprise. To that end, five major focus areas have emerged:

---

[2] Report of the Secretary of Defense Task Force on DoD Nuclear Weapons Management Phase I: The Air Force's Nuclear Mission, September 2008.

- Restore the culture of compliance

- Rebuild our nuclear expertise

- Invest in our nuclear capabilities

- Organize to enable clear lines of authority providing sustained institutional focus

- Reinvigorate our Air Force nuclear stewardship role

Culture of Compliance

The Air Force will rebuild a **nuclear culture of compliance** that reflects robust inspection processes under the independent oversight of the SAF/IG. All assessments and inspections will apply common standards derived from inputs of all stakeholders to effectively uncover, analyze, address, and review systemic weaknesses within our nuclear enterprise. This overarching goal is achievable, but will require the combined efforts of leaders and multiple organizations committed to these objectives. Leadership at all levels must make nuclear mission oversight and self-assessment a priority. Leaders must take ownership and responsibility for assessments, be self-critical and enforce accountability. At the same time, leaders must support regular cross-talk activity at all levels.

Nuclear Expertise

We will **rebuild our expertise** through Air Force-wide training, education, and career force development initiatives designed to ensure that we create a basic atmosphere of understanding for our nuclear stewardship responsibilities. The nuclear enterprise must have properly trained, seasoned nuclear professionals focusing on the daily deterrence mission. These initiatives will be driven by senior leadership involvement and oversight of force development of the nuclear enterprise.

Investment

We will provide needed **investments** and resources for this vital mission area. The Air Force must invest in the nuclear deterrence mission and have a clear, long-term commitment to sustain, modernize, and recapitalize its nuclear capability. Based upon national guidance and vetted combatant command and major command requirements, the Air Force Corporate Structure (AFCS) process will recommend the proper balance of capability and risk to senior leadership to ensure funding decisions are based upon relevant, accurate, consistent, defendable, repeatable, and transparent data and analysis. These funding decisions must be made with a full understanding of the implications for the Air Force nuclear enterprise. In addition, the requirements, acquisition, and programming processes must be aligned to provide a solid program baseline and acquisition strategy to minimize the cost, schedule, and performance risks inherent in delivering reliable and modern operational systems/capabilities to preserve the Air Force portion of our Nation's nuclear capability.

Organization

We will create a **composite operational, sustainment, and headquarters organizational structure** that concentrates nuclear mission oversight in order to dramatically improve focus and provide clear lines of authority for the nuclear mission. Success in rebuilding the nuclear enterprise can only be achieved when certain imperatives are realized: restoring confidence and credibility; elevating the importance of the mission; Airmen are consistently held accountable for their performance; and the Air Force commits itself as an enduring provider of two legs of the nation's nuclear deterrent forces. The composite organizational construct will be an enabler for these imperatives.

Nuclear Stewardship

Finally, we will **restore our allies' and public's confidence in our nuclear stewardship role** through accomplishing the actions identified in this roadmap. These actions will ensure we have the right culture, the right people, the right investments, and the right organizational structure in place to ensure the Air Force provides widely recognized and respected capabilities with the intended strategic effect: enduring nuclear deterrence.

Summary of Key Actions

To effectively reinvigorate the nuclear enterprise, the Air Force must undertake a series of root cause-based action plans that implement the objectives of restoring the culture of compliance and exacting adherence to standards; rebuilding our expertise base; investing in our nuclear capabilities; effectively organizing around a composite operational, sustainment, and headquarters construct; and securing public confidence in our stewardship role through an integrated set of measurable implementation plans and processes.

In summary, the roadmap is a "contract for change." Contained within the 100 action items is a composite set of major actions that define the essence of the roadmap and, in aggregate, represent a bold step forward. The following is a summary of the major actions required:

- Consolidate all nuclear sustainment functions under AFMC/AFNWC. (OPR: AFMC, create Mission Directive, by Apr 09)

- Establish positive inventory control measures for nuclear weapons-related materiel. (OPR: AF/A4/7, modify AFMAN 23-110, AFI 21-203 and create applicable new AFRs, by Apr 09)

- Enhance Nuclear Inspection processes: establish an AF-wide inspector training and certification program; implement independent oversight of all command-level NSIs by SAF/IG; establish a centrally managed core team of highly experienced NSI inspectors; establish procedures for adjudicating discrepancies between MAJCOM and oversight teams (these procedures will be approved by the Nuclear Oversight Board); and recommend to the Nuclear Oversight Board how

AF nuclear inspection processes might be further improved, including whether Nuclear Surety Inspections (NSI) should be SAF/IG led or remain MAJCOM-led. (OPR: SAF/IG, recommendations to the NOB by Dec 08, modify AFI 90-201, by Apr 09)

- Align strategic deterrence/nuclear operations-based education, training, career development and force development activities. (OPR: AF/A1, modify AFI 36-2302, AFI 36-2640, by Apr 09)

- Increase nuclear mission focus, by placing all ICBMs and nuclear-capable bombers into a single command: establish Air Force Global Strike Command. (OPR: AF/A3/5N, stand up Provisional HQ, by Dec 08; write PAD 08-04, by Dec 08; stand up MAJCOM, by Sep 09)

- Increase USAF institutional nuclear focus, policy oversight, integration and establish air staff nuclear accountable officer: establish AF/A10. (OPR: AF/A3/5N, stand up NLT 1 Nov 08)

- Improve nuclear stewardship in AF corporate processes: Consolidate nuclear-related Program Elements into one panel or a similarly robust management portfolio; revise Group, Board, Panel and Council structure; develop a beta-test nuclear enterprise virtual Major Force Program (vMFP). (OPR: AF/A8, modify AFI 16-501) (by Dec 08)

- Create strategic plans that address long-term nuclear requirements…Cruise Missile; Bomber; DCA; ICBM. (OPR: AF/A8, modify AFI 16-501)

- Charge the Under Secretary of the Air Force with ongoing broad policy and oversight responsibilities for nuclear matters.

- The Secretary of the Air Force establishes policy for nuclear matters. The SecAF and CSAF will jointly chair the Air Force Nuclear Oversight Board (NOB) which shall meet at least quarterly to resolve outstanding issues, and specifically to: 1.) oversee implementation of this roadmap, and report progress to SECDEF and Congress; 2.) review nuclear policies, standards, performance metrics, and compliance; and 3.) ensure continuing effective stewardship of the Air Force nuclear enterprise. (OPR: AF/A10 establish NOB NLT Nov 08)

Conclusion

Nuclear forces continue to represent the ultimate deterrence capability that supports U.S. national security. Because of their immense destructive power, nuclear weapons, as recognized in the 2006 National Security Strategy, deter in a way that simply cannot be duplicated by other weapons. Additionally, the special nature of nuclear weapons demands precise performance across the Air Force nuclear enterprise, with no tolerance for complacency or shortcuts. In short, we will continue to fortify current operations, develop our people, and sustain and modernize current capabilities.

This roadmap is the foundation for reinvigorating the Air Force nuclear enterprise and to re-establish the confidence in our ability to provide nuclear deterrence for our nation and our allies.

The American people depend on the United States Air Force to deliver precise and reliable nuclear deterrence capabilities and have done so for over 61 years. America's Airmen accept this mission with pride, professionalism and a solemn commitment to the hallmark standards of excellence of the United States Air Force. We will make this important work a success.

Chapter 1 — Introduction

A credible nuclear deterrent is essential to our security and that of our allies and friends. The Air Force has an essential role in this national mission. We were created as a separate service over 60 years ago with nuclear responsibilities foremost in our mission set. There is no mission more sensitive than safeguarding our vital nuclear capabilities and maintaining nuclear deterrence. We have a sacred trust with the American people to safely operate, maintain, and secure nuclear weapons. We must constantly strive for perfection in this mission area. Rigid adherence to standards, personal accountability at all levels, and leadership are the foundations upon which our success depends.

Honorable Michael B. Donley, 26 June 2008

Purpose of the Air Force Nuclear Enterprise Roadmap

This roadmap is a contract for change, containing approximately 100 action items that are designed as building blocks for the combined governance, structure, and cultural foundation. It contains comprehensive action plans that describe the actions required to restore public trust and ensure a credible nuclear deterrence. It also advocates the institutional way ahead to regenerate the culture of absolute excellence and develop trained and prepared Airmen to execute the extraordinary and unique demands of nuclear operations.

This document focuses primarily on the stewardship of the nuclear mission from an operational level. Major commands (MAJCOMs) are expected to create follow-on documents, specific to their commands, from this roadmap. Concepts of Employment (CONEMPs), tactics, threats, and capabilities are also not discussed in this document. These topics should also be explored and defined by the MAJCOMs.

The Department of the Air Force is responsible by Congressional statute to organize, train, and equip our nuclear forces to ensure effective nuclear deterrence and flawless nuclear surety. This roadmap provides fundamental guidance on how to better organize, train, and equip our nuclear forces to ensure effective nuclear deterrence and flawless nuclear surety. We must rebuild a culture that embraces the importance and criticality of the nuclear deterrence mission, conveys our credibility and commitment to potential adversaries and our mission partners, and creates an atmosphere in which all Airmen understand and value the Air Force nuclear mission. We are committed to improving our headquarters, sustainment, and operational organizational construct to enable coherent lines of authority, drive institutional focus, and ensure unambiguous accountability for the nuclear mission.

This roadmap aims to identify common actions that must be standardized to ensure safe, secure, and reliable nuclear operations. The action plans will be underpinned by organizational change that better enables day-to-day excellence throughout the Air

Force nuclear enterprise and clearly aligns mission focus with that of the combatant commanders it supports. The strategic action plans guide and leverage the scores of associated and cascading action items directed in this roadmap and form the foundation of an implementation strategy that is action-focused, timely, and measurable with clear accountable leads for each plan.

- (Leadership) SecAF will establish Air Force Nuclear Oversight Board to oversee implementation of this roadmap and report progress to SECDEF and Congress. This Board will ensure enduring stewardship of the nuclear enterprise. The Board will be jointly chaired by SecAF and CSAF. Members include USecAF, VCSAF, Nuclear MAJCOM Commanders, AFNWC/CC, SAF/GC, AF/JA, SAF/IG, AF/A10, and other members as designated by SecAF

Ongoing USAF Commitments / Global Challenges / Expectations

We remain committed to fighting terrorism, sustaining our current joint operations, assuring our allies, and adapting our ability to detect, deter, dissuade, and defeat adversaries to protect America and achieve national objectives. America's Airmen are battle-tested and have proven capabilities applicable and adaptable across the entire spectrum of conflict. Today's Global War on Terror (GWOT) missions are only the latest in a string of more than 18 years of continuous combat, beginning with our initial Operation DESERT SHIELD deployments in August 1990. Years of persistent conflict in Southwest Asia, Somalia, Bosnia, Serbia, Kosovo, Haiti, and around the globe represent a dramatic change from military operations during the Cold War.

Today's Air Force provides the Joint Force Commander a range of capabilities that set conditions for success. We apply agility, reach, speed, stealth, payload, firepower, precision, and persistence to achieve global effects. Dominance of air, space, and cyberspace domains provide the essential foundation for effective joint operations. To achieve these capabilities, our Airmen currently fly approximately 430 sorties daily as part of OIF and OEF, including inter-theater and intra-theater airlift; aeromedical evacuation (AE); aerial refueling; command, control, communications, computers, intelligence, surveillance, and reconnaissance (C4ISR); strike; close air support (CAS); and electronic warfare (EW).

Since 2001, the active duty Air Force further reduced its end-strength by almost 6%, but our deployments have increased by at least 30% – primarily in support of the GWOT. In addition to the 25,000 Airmen deployed to CENTCOM's AOR at any one time, approximately 213,000 Airmen (183,000 active duty plus an additional 30,000 Guard and Reserve) fulfill other daily combatant commander requirements, missions and tasks 24 hours a day, seven days a week. Approximately 40% of our total force (including 53% of the active duty force) is globally and directly engaged. From controlling satellites to flying unmanned aerial systems (UASs), from standing on strategic missile alert to parsing intelligence information, Airmen directly engage America's adversaries and influence events worldwide every day.

To accomplish our increasing, diverse taskings, many of our Airmen require a great deal of additional training. Such extra training means even more time away from units already stretched thin by the Air Force's high operational tempo (OPSTEMPO) and force drawdown. Because deployed units and Airmen are no longer available for core Air Force or home-station missions, and because our core missions must still be accomplished, the workload shifts to other Airmen at home and abroad. In addition, Airmen's skills in their core competencies are perishable, and we must give them time for training to hone those skills.

Within this challenging and dynamic environment, the Air Force will nurture a professional nuclear force, ensure we are postured to deter potential adversaries, employ upon Presidential direction, and support allies in ways that strengthen US national security.

Changes in the Strategic Environment

Over the past two decades, radical changes in the strategic environment shaped the Air Force nuclear enterprise and affected nuclear enterprise-related decisions. Through analysis, a common set of strategic root causes emerged:

- The Cold War victory led to substantial arms reductions and changes to the National Security Strategy, de-emphasizing the importance of nuclear weapons in the strategic deterrence mission

- In 1992, the Air Force implemented the largest organizational change since its inception that led to the organizational and authoritative fragmentation of the Air Force nuclear enterprise

- Military down-sizing since the end of the Cold War, specifically in organizations that were part of the nuclear mission, has fragmented nuclear sustainment and reduced the pool of nuclear expertise

- Since 1992, the Air Force reduced the priority to invest in some nuclear mission areas, and modernization or recapitalization of some systems in the Air Force nuclear enterprise was extremely limited

- Air Force concepts of operations evolved to emphasize new missions and capabilities that began to overshadow nuclear operations. Advancement of Air Force contributions to Joint and Composite Force operations increased focus on expeditionary operations and a renewed emphasis in irregular warfare

Air Force Commitment to Rebuild Public Trust

The Air Force must ensure we have national trust and confidence in our institutional ability to organize, train, and equip professional nuclear forces across the spectrum of peacetime and wartime missions. In order to accomplish this overarching purpose, the Air Force must revitalize enterprise-wide efforts with a specific set of priorities outlined in this roadmap. We have a sacred trust with our Nation to safely maintain and secure nuclear weapons while maintaining the capability to employ them effectively, if directed by the President. Therefore, we must maintain flawless nuclear weapons safety, security, and reliability and readiness programs. The Air Force brings unique capabilities to the nation's nuclear deterrence posture: a robust alert force comprised of Minuteman III Intercontinental Ballistic Missiles (ICBM) and bomber and fighter forces comprised of B-52, B-2, and dual-capable aircraft (DCA) fighters that provide our nation and our allies the ability to visibly signal our resolve to potential adversaries by aircraft movement and generation.

Definition of Air Force Nuclear Enterprise

The Air Force nuclear enterprise consists of the people, organizations, processes, procedures, and systems that are used to conduct, execute, and support nuclear operations and forces. It includes the infrastructure and life-cycle activities for nuclear weapons, delivery platforms, and supporting systems; intellectual and technical competencies; and cultural mindset that ensure sustainable, responsive, safe, reliable, and secure Air Force nuclear deterrence capabilities. In addition, it includes Air Force organizations responsible for nuclear policy and guidance, and Air Force relationships with other entities who contribute to the Nation's nuclear deterrence mission.

Attributes of a Successful Air Force Nuclear Enterprise

Air Force leadership must clearly and consistently emphasize the premium our nation puts on strategic deterrence and the vital contribution the AF makes in this mission area. These words must be reinforced by actions, to include robust training and rigorous adherence to standards that is measurable and repeatable. The Air Force nuclear enterprise systems and processes require redundancies and safeguards to achieve fail-safe operations. There is no tolerance for complacency or shortcuts as we rebuild a "zero-defect" culture. Our culture of reliability, adherence to standards, and rigorous self-assessment relies on constant, realistic training and exercises combined with robust inspections. However, inspection is not the end state—it is a means to provide the feedback necessary to continuously improve processes and performance. In addition to training, exercises, and inspection, the Air Force nuclear enterprise relies on meticulous systems engineering and operational safety, suitability, and effectiveness (OSS&E) processes. Nuclear Weapon System Operational Safety Reviews and the safety design certification process are crucial to ensure AF compliance with the four DoD Nuclear Weapon System Safety Standards. Additionally, it relies on true enterprise management tools to ensure the reliability of the entire system. Furthermore, the Air Force requires advocacy for all aspects of the nuclear mission, both inside and outside the Air Force. Finally, our investment in the Air Force nuclear enterprise must be sufficient to safely, securely, and reliably sustain current requirements as well as meet future modernization and recapitalization requirements.

Atrophy of the USAF Nuclear Enterprise

Recent incidents highlighted breakdowns in the Air Force nuclear enterprise and pointed to systemic weaknesses. In response to these incidents and the subsequent investigations and studies, the Air Force created the Air Force Nuclear Task Force (AFNTF). The AFNTF was comprised of nuclear experts from across the enterprise and charged with comprehensively evaluating and consolidating findings and recommendations from the *Commander Directed Investigation Concerning an*

Unauthorized Transfer of Nuclear Warheads, 30 August 2007 (CDI); *Blue Ribbon Review of Nuclear Weapons Policies and Procedures,* 8 February 2008 (BRR); *The Defense Science Board* (DSB) *Permanent Task Force on Nuclear Weapons Surety – Report on Unauthorized Movement of Nuclear Weapons, April 2008; Air Force Inventory and Assessment: Nuclear Weapons and Nuclear Weapons-Related Materiel, 25 May 2008 (AFRIT); Admiral (ADM) Donald Investigation into the Shipment of Sensitive Missile Components to Taiwan, 22 May 2008* (ADM Donald Report); and the *Air Force Comprehensive Assessment of Nuclear Sustainment Report , July 2008* (CANS). In addition, the AFNTF reviewed and incorporated results from the recently completed *Report of the Secretary of Defense Task Force on DoD Nuclear Weapons Management, Phase I: the Air Force's Nuclear Mission,* September 2008 (Schlesinger Report). The Air Force nuclear enterprise roadmap, *Reinvigorating the Air Force Nuclear Enterprise,* is the product of these investigations and internal assessments. The reports converged on six recurring themes to focus our revitalization efforts:

- Rebuild a culture of accountability and rigorous self-assessment dedicated to high standards of excellence in the Air Force nuclear enterprise

- Rebuild nuclear expertise and codify career paths

- Construct an end-to-end Air Force nuclear sustainment enterprise system and revitalize the sustainment community

- Develop a comprehensive investment plan committed to meeting the requirements of the nuclear deterrence mission

- Create an environment of sustained advocacy for the nuclear deterrence mission

- Align authorities and responsibilities for nuclear deterrence mission requirements

Roadmap Organization

Each chapter in this roadmap addresses one of the themes listed above. Each chapter includes a problem statement, root causes, attributes of success, objectives, and action plans. During action plan development, the AFNTF applied a Doctrine, Organization, Training, Materiel, Leadership and Education, Personnel, and Facilities (DOTMLPF) approach to each specific task in order to build a comprehensive solution set. Below is a brief definition of the DOTMLPF Change Recommendation (DCR) process, listed in Chairman Joint Chiefs of Staff Instruction (CJCSI) 3170.1:

- Doctrine – The way we fight (in addition to traditional doctrine, the category includes Air Force Instructions (AFIs), policies, and guidance)

- Organization – How we organize to fight (includes staff and support)

- Training – How we prepare our people (basic training to joint exercises)

- Materiel – All things necessary to equip our forces

- Leadership and education – How we prepare out leaders to lead the fight from squad leader to 4-star general/admiral; professional military education (PME)

- Personnel – Availability of qualified people for peacetime, wartime, and contingency operations

- Facilities – Real property, installations, and industrial facilities

Each action lists the DOTMLPF approach, OPR, action plan description, associated report findings (with finding text outlined in Appendix 4), timeline, and policy and guidance references. These actions, and their supporting detailed (tactical) actions, are tracked and managed in the Nuclear Enterprise Management Tool (NEMT) described in Appendix 3. Air Staff and MAJCOM OPRs are responsible for both the actions outlined in the Roadmap and the supporting actions maintained in the NEMT.

Chapter Summaries

Re-establish a Culture of Accountability and Rigorous Self-Assessment

To restore a culture of compliance and rigid adherence to standards, Secretary of the Air Force Inspector General (SAF/IG) will implement centralized, independent oversight over Air Force nuclear inspections and assessments, while preserving MAJCOM organize, train, and equip authorities and responsibilities. It will ensure common inspection standards that will include consistent inspection policy, accurate functional guidance, and standardized checklists; expanding oversight of all Nuclear Surety Inspections by SAF/IG, USSTRATCOM, or Defense Threat Reduction Agency (DTRA), and establishing a cadre of experienced nuclear surety inspectors at the Air Force Inspection Agency (AFIA) for participation in nuclear inspections. SAF/IG will also establish procedures for reporting and adjudicating discrepancies between inspection teams and oversight authorities for Nuclear Oversight Board (NOB) approval.

Rebuild Nuclear Expertise

To overcome the erosion of nuclear expertise, the Air Force set forth a path to examine education and training across the enterprise, improve identification and tracking of nuclear experience and expertise, and establish a force development governance construct to ensure continual, formalized senior leadership involvement in the development of future nuclear leaders.

The Air Force Manpower, Personnel, and Services (AF/A1), in conjunction with Air University (AU) and a panel of functional and major command representatives, reviewed the complete spectrum of officer and enlisted PME. The full scope of formal training courses, some taught within the Air Education and Training Command (AETC) structure and some outside, was also reviewed. Inspection and evaluation criteria are being developed by Air Force training experts for non-AETC courses to ensure consistency and adherence to training objectives.

Key nuclear billets have been formally identified and Special Experience Identifiers (SEIs) developed and assigned to ensure individuals filling key positions posses the

14

required background and experiences to effectively lead the nuclear enterprise. Identifying key billets outside of standard AF organizations (e.g., Dept of Energy, DTRA, etc.) will broaden the expertise and experience of Air Force nuclear leaders.

Finally, senior leadership involvement in developing nuclear leaders will be institutionalized through the Nuclear Enterprise Advisory Panel (NEAP). The NEAP, chaired by the new AF/A10 (AF/A3/5N), serves as a cross functional review and advisory panel to the Force Management and Development Council (FMDC) chaired by the Vice Chief of Staff of the Air Force. The NEAP will provide force development oversight for officers, enlisted, and civilian personnel -- those within purely nuclear career fields and those in supporting, and equally important, roles.

The combination and maturation of these efforts addressing education and training, identifying and tracking nuclear expertise, and formal senior leadership oversight of nuclear force development is designed to reverse the erosion of nuclear skills and expertise within the Air Force. More work remains to be done, but the Air Force has already moved forward and shown commitment to rebuilding expertise in the nuclear enterprise.

Security expertise is a common thread for all personnel associated with nuclear weapons and a key piece of the nuclear enterprise. Although security was not associated with specific findings, Appendix 5 of this roadmap outlines our efforts to improve security performance. Additionally, AETC will expand its current responsibilities from providing initial training to include mission-specific training for security duty at nuclear-capable wings.

Sustainment

The Air Force will organize nuclear sustainment with clear lines of authority and responsibility, comprehensive logistics and supply chain management (SCM), fail-safe maintenance, inventory, and distribution processes, responsive engineering support, and robust and comprehensive training at all levels. To achieve these standards, the Air Force must reestablish a clear and focused organizational structure. Nuclear weapons-related materiel (NWRM) must be defined and subsequently treated with extra levels of control and oversight. Units responsible for handling NWRM must be appropriately equipped with personnel, tools, infrastructure and guidance to establish and maintain an auditable, standardized positive inventory control system for all such materiel. Fail-safe logistics processes and engineering support throughout the Air Force nuclear enterprise must be documented, attributable, and authored by a cognizant engineering authority. Finally, the Air Force must institute robust and comprehensive training programs for nuclear sustainment at all levels, including oversight and assessment.

Investment: Requirements, Acquisition, and Programming

To ensure appropriate, sustained institutional commitment to the Air Force nuclear enterprise and Air Force nuclear-related capability, mid- and long-range planning and programming strategies must be refined.

AF/A8, with inputs from appropriate MAJCOMs and Air Force Council deliberation, will create strategic plans that address Air Force mid-term requirements (i.e., F-35 dual capability, tanker replacement, and weapons storage area (WSA) alignment), and long-term requirements and acquisition strategies to ensure future viability of our nuclear deterrent forces (i.e., weapons, delivery systems, communications, and supporting infrastructure).

AF/A8 has refined the headquarters Air Force (HAF) corporate process by assigning AF/A10 (AF/A3/5N) to the Air Force Group and Board. In addition, AF/A8 will continue the evaluation of the portfolios of the existing 12 panels of the AFCS to identify Program Elements (PE) which directly or indirectly impact and comprise the Air Force nuclear enterprise; continue the evaluation of consolidating all nuclear-related PEs into one panel, or a similarly robust management portfolio; and evaluate a "beta-test" virtual Major Force Program dedicated to the Air Force nuclear enterprise in order to consolidate all nuclear-related programs into one robust management and data repository.

Advocacy Across the Air Force Nuclear Enterprise

Air Force senior leaders, through concerted actions and communications focused on the nuclear mission, will drive advocacy for the Air Force's nuclear enterprise. This will ensure nuclear education and training is valued and will emphasize the importance of the nuclear mission to all Airmen. Finally, the Air Force will build a cadre of experts who can engage and influence combatant command, joint force and Office of the Secretary of Defense policy and guidance regarding the nuclear mission and relate the uniqueness and importance of the nuclear mission in overarching national strategy and operational plans.

To communicate the Air Force commitment to re-invigorating the Air Force nuclear enterprise, Secretary of the Air Force Directorate of Communication and Public Affairs, in coordination with the Special Assistant for Air Force Strategy, AF/A8, AF/A10 (AF/A3/5N), and MAJCOM CCs, will create a coordinated, advocacy-based engagement strategy that enables thoughtful Air Force input to national and joint policy, strategy and planning processes, and puts the Air Force on notice that real, enduring changes and improvements are needed throughout the Air Force nuclear enterprise.

Organizational Alternatives

After analyzing several courses of action (COAs), the Air Force has further consolidated its nuclear sustainment activities under AFMC, specifically AFNWC, which is consistent with Dr. Schlesinger's Task Force Report recommendations. Under this COA, the commander of AFMC is responsible for consolidated sustainment of Air Force nuclear weapons and nuclear weapons-related materiel.

The Air Force considered several reorganization alternatives to reinvigorate the nuclear enterprise as part of the roadmap development. The field operations organization attributes used to develop, analyze, and compare the organizational alternatives were derived from the previously mentioned SECDEF directed reports and studies, as well as inputs from nuclear MAJCOM staffs. During the Fall 2008 CORONA Conference, it was decided to establish a new major command (Air Force Global Strike Command) focused on and dedicated to the nuclear deterrence and global strike missions.

At the Nuclear Summit held 18 September 2008, a decision was made to create a new AF/A10 headquarters directorate. The establishment of the AF/A10 sends a clear and visible signal that the Air Force is committed to resolving the fragmented lines of authority across all levels of the nuclear enterprise and provides a headquarters Assistant Chief of Staff that reports directly to the CSAF with authority to drive nuclear enterprise policy, guidance, requirements, and advocacy across the HAF staff. The AF/A10 will be the single HAF authority for all nuclear related issues and will have lead responsibilities for nuclear operations, plans, policy, and requirements.

Assessment

The action plan assessment processes identify and measure assessment metrics that display the progress made toward reinvigorating the nuclear enterprise and meeting strategic objectives such as rebuilding a culture of rigorous self-assessment or rebuilding expertise in the Air Force nuclear enterprise. This is accomplished through the development of measures of performance (MOP) and measures of effectiveness (MOE). These measures require agreement of subject matter experts (SMEs) and leadership throughout the enterprise and those most involved with the mission. These measures will ensure a precise and objective assessment of the enterprise's health and highlight areas in which additional progress is still required. (See Appendix 2 – Methodology for greater detail).

Summary

Nuclear weapons, along with the operations, support, maintenance, infrastructure, and security associated with them, are a unique national capability. The destructive power of nuclear weapons and their political effects places them under the direct control of the President. Nuclear operations are the linchpin of strategic deterrence. Their flexibility provides decision space to the President to exercise escalation control measures, demonstrate resolve, negotiate with authority, assure friends and allies, ensure US national security against disruptive technological challenges, and defeat adversaries with prompt, overwhelming force.

As stated in Dr. Schlesinger's Task Force Report, "Because nuclear weapons have been less prominent since the end of the Cold War and have not been used since World War II, their importance and unique role as a deterrent have been obscured, but not diminished. Though our consistent goal has been to avoid actual weapons use, the nuclear deterrent is "used" every day by assuring friends and allies, dissuading opponents from seeking peer capabilities to the United States, deterring attacks on the United States and its allies from potential adversaries, and providing the potential to defeat adversaries if deterrence fails."[3]

---

[3] Report of the Secretary of Defense Task Force on DoD Nuclear Weapons Management Phase I: The Air Force's Nuclear Mission, September 2008, Page 1.

Our existing national military strategy (NMS) addresses the importance of nuclear weapons in deterring a wide range of threats, not just nuclear attacks. During the Cold War, the potential destructive power of nuclear weapons helped to prevent war between great powers. In the emerging international security environment, nuclear weapons will continue to play a major role in deterring the use of weapons of mass destruction (WMD) and large-scale conventional attacks against US vital interests. Moreover, the United States extends its nuclear security umbrella in support of our allies and our common vital interests. US extended deterrence also mitigates incentives for allies to develop their own nuclear weapons programs and deploy independent nuclear forces.

The probability of a chemical, biological, radiological, and/or nuclear (CBRN) attack against the US or its interests has increased since the end of the Cold War. Rogue nation-states and terrorist groups seeking to develop and/or acquire WMDs are enabled and motivated by technology transfers, surrogate resourcing, misplaced phobias, and posturing for attention within the international community. The US, its allies, and like-minded nations, fully aware of the growing threat, must determine how to deter such attacks and protect their interests. To this end, the strategic deterrence provided by the US nuclear enterprise is vital in preventing the proliferation of WMD by our allies and its use by our enemies. The Air Force has a responsibility to recognize and embrace the indispensable role of nuclear weapons in strategic deterrence and its role on US nonproliferation efforts.

Regardless of the size of the US nuclear arsenal, the continued development of foreign nuclear capabilities and the uncertain political trajectories of potential US adversaries, our enduirng responsibility is the effective stewardship of our nuclear enterprise. Related to these conditions, the DSB Task Force on Nuclear Weapons Surety stated: "Those are the only facts needed to understand the requirement for sustained, intense attention to the nuclear enterprise and to robust nuclear weapons surety."

— Re-establish a Culture of Accountability and Rigorous Self-Assessment

> *"... We must build a wider understanding of the importance of deterrence and the logic of building forces that deter effectively...it is a major undertaking."*
>
> *Larry Welch, Gen (ret) 12th CSAF*

Problem Statement

The Air Force lacks clear accountability and effective processes to identify and correct systemic weaknesses through its inspection and self-assessment programs.

Success Criteria and Desired Sub-Objectives

The Air Force will rebuild a nuclear culture that has a robust self-assessment and inspection process in order to effectively uncover, analyze, address, and review systemic weaknesses within its nuclear enterprise. This overarching goal is achievable, but will require the combined efforts of leaders and organizations committed to these objectives.

Combatant commands should commit to clear requirements regarding the nuclear mission and the Air Force. The Air Force, along with our joint partners, should revise Technical Order (T.O.) 11N-25-1 to provide clear guidance on nuclear inspection criteria.

Quality assurance (QA) activities must have clear guidance, standardized processes and criteria, and certified QA evaluators. Unit commanders must actively manage vigorous self-inspection programs. In addition, the Air Force must have standardized training, qualification, and certification requirements for all inspection team members, establish common checklists, employ root cause analysis (RCA), improve overall trend analysis for systemic issues, and instill rigor in tracking findings to closure. Unit commanders must implement and encourage a day-to-day culture of self-assessment whereby unit members routinely use root cause analysis methodologies to identify the root cause of problems and deficiencies as they are discovered.

Leadership at all levels must make nuclear mission oversight and self-assessment their highest priority. Air Force leaders failed in their leadership responsibilities to shift priorities and adjust policies and resources in ways needed to maintain robust nuclear stewardship, resulting in the inattention that led to the Minot-Barksdale and Taiwan incidents. Leaders must take ownership and responsibility for assessments, be self-critical, and enforce accountability. At the same time, leaders must support regular cross-talk activity at all levels.

To restore a culture of compliance and rigid adherence to standards, SAF/IG will implement centralized, independent oversight over Air Force nuclear inspections and assessments while preserving MAJCOM authorities and responsibilities for training and readiness of their assigned forces. It will ensure common inspection standards, consistent inspection policy, accurate functional guidance, and standardized checklists. SAF/IG will establish a cadre of experienced nuclear surety inspectors at AFIA for participation in nuclear inspections. SAF/IG will continue to work with the DTRA to establish a common understanding and application of Nuclear Surety Inspection (NSI) criteria. SAF/IG will also establish procedures for reporting and adjudicating discrepancies between inspection teams and oversight authorities for Nuclear Oversight Board (NOB) approval that will ensure the nuclear inspection process is accountable, independent, and transparent to outside review.

Root Causes

Weaknesses in Nuclear Inspections, Staff Assistance Visits and Unit Quality Assurance Programs

The Air Force nuclear inspections, nuclear surety staff assistance visits, and unit quality assurance programs are not consistent across MAJCOMs or agencies supporting and/or inspecting the nuclear enterprise. The ADM Donald Report identified oversight, inspections, and internal audits as ineffective in resolving recurring deficiencies and highlighted ineffective follow-up to ensure identified problems were adequately addressed.

Inspection weaknesses include:

- Non-standardized and insufficient metrics to identify trends or inadequate trend analysis to drive process improvements (weakness in causal analysis and corrective actions in response to deficiencies identified during inspections) (ADM Donald Report)

- Deficiencies documented as minor potentially indicated more systemic problems associated with compliance or training, resulting in narrow corrective actions associated with specific findings rather than a recognition of more fundamental problems (ADM Donald Report)

- Air Force Instruction (AFI) 90-201 cause code for all findings lacks sufficient detail to enable thorough analysis and identification of long-term corrective actions to correct root issue (ADM Donald Report)

- Inconsistent documentation of identified deficiencies limited the ability to recognize trends across similar maintenance activities (CANS)

- Inconsistent practices to capture and implement best practices between units (ADM Donald Report)

Nuclear Surety Staff Assistance Visit (NSSAV) weaknesses include:

20

- Lack of common NSSAV processes across all nuclear MAJCOMs, NAFs, and Centers (ADM Donald Report, BRR)

- Lack of formal system to track observations and lack of follow-up to ensure deficiencies were resolved (ADM Donald Report)

- Lack of timely, formal crosstalk between wing leadership after staff assistance visit (SAVs) to identify issues or highlight best practices (ADM Donald Report)

- Lack of statistical rigor to identify trends and potential root causes (CANS)

Quality Assurance issues include:

- Nonexistent quality assurance evaluation criteria to ensure high standards (ADM Donald Report)

- Some functional compliance checklists are stove-piped. Individual unit task checklists are narrowly focused and not adequately tied to unit checklists (ADM Donald Report)

- Deficiencies often binned into general categories, limiting trending ability (does not address potential underlying causes of the deficiency or identify corrective actions to address deficiencies) (ADM Donald Report)

- Deficiencies identified and corrected by technicians and supervisors are not documented or captured for future trend analysis (ADM Donald Report)

Unit Self-Inspection issues include:

- No formalized training within unit self-inspection programs (Schlesinger Report)

- Deficiencies corrected within 5-days of identification are not entered into databases. This results in a sparse database and limits trend analysis or identifying potential command-wide problems (ADM Donald Report)

Inadequate, Insufficient, and Conflicting Policy and Guidance

Inadequate, insufficient, and conflicting guidance and policy from Air Force, MAJCOMs and combatant commands have created a variety of challenges for the Air Force nuclear enterprise. In some cases, combatant command priorities and taskings have limited mission performance evaluations during Nuclear Operational Readiness Inspections (NORIs).

A number of nuclear policies, procedures, and processes affecting nuclear operations are confusing and non-standard. Policy and guidance issues include:

- Leadership does not adequately review or update nuclear policy and guidance (BRR)

- Non-standard oversight and assessment processes for nuclear activities including external and internal inspections/SAVs across the Air Force nuclear enterprise (IG, SAVs, QA, unit self-inspection) (ADM Donald Report)

- Absence of a process to harmonize interpretations of T.O. 11N-25-1, Department of Defense *(DoD) Nuclear Weapons Technical Inspection System,* between Air Force and the Office of the Secretary of Defense (OSD)/DTRA has resulted in grading disagreements (BRR)

- Lack of governing policy for managing nuclear weapons-related materiel (NWRM); also insufficient definition of NWRM (CANS)

- Lack of Air Force-level inspection checklists (CANS)

- Non-standardized nuclear inspection processes and subjective grading criteria has reduced efficiencies and created confusion; Initial Nuclear Surety Inspection (INSI) guidance needs improvement and unit certification/decertification guidance requires formalization (BRR, CANS)

- Incomplete guidance on accountability of nuclear certified equipment (CANS)

- Inadequate weapon technical order guidance prevalent (ADM Donald Report)

- Current Air Force Instructions are interpreted as being less directive than prior year's Air Force Regulations (AFRs) (August 2008 GreyBeard Panel Report)

Culture of Accountability Eroded
- Over time, handling bomber nuclear weapons has come to be regarded as an exercise activity rather than a serious operational activity (DSB)

- Bomber nuclear exercises are not meeting current requirements in frequency or scale (BRR)

- Key nuclear leadership billets are filled by personnel who do not have nuclear experience or depth (BRR)

- Dispersed lines of authority contributed to a loss of systems engineering discipline within the ICBM program (CANS)

Erosion of Rigid Adherence to Standards and "Zero Defect" Culture
Nuclear missions are unique and require a "zero defect" culture. However, the Air Force embraced a "risk management" mindset. The continuing drive for efficiencies outweighed redundant checks and inspections that identify deficiencies or errors before they became critical. Often, individuals focused on quickly correcting the symptoms of failure rather than identifying core weaknesses and implementing enduring solutions.

Air Force leadership and supervisors failed to communicate in actions and words the enormous responsibility associated with the nuclear mission. Conflicting or limited/non-existent guidance further eroded a rigid adherence to standards. Inadequate supervision and training and limited accountability all contributed to the Air Force diversion from a nuclear "zero defect" culture. Findings include:

- Failure to adhere to established policies coupled with multiple independent data/messaging systems caused confusion and consumed time and resources (CANS)

- Informal technical guidance issued (contrary to technical order guidance) (ADM Donald Report)

- Confusion over the applicability of nuclear weapons handling procedures for nuclear weapon systems that do not contain nuclear warheads (DSB)

- Lack of clear and detailed direction in instructions and technical orders particularly in light of a less experienced workforce (BRR)

- Air Force nuclear-related inspection processes do not emphasize or assess the quality of self-assessment performed by inspected commands (ADM Donald Report)

- ADM Donald's investigation identified long-term supply chain process failures and weaknesses that indicated systemic issues had not been corrected (ADM Donald Report)

Loss of Nuclear Focus

Findings identified that limited nuclear focus built a culture of disinterest and apathy rather than the required culture of critical self-assessment.

- The various levels of inspection activities have failed to detect changes in process which compromised established procedures (DSB)

- Leadership does not adequately oversee or review nuclear sustainment areas. A review found little officer engagement in the execution of maintenance work—little formal or visible supervision of the work by responsible officers. (ADM Donald Report, CANS)

- Focus on the nuclear mission, especially in dual-capable bomber units, has diminished from the robust nuclear culture that existed during the Cold War (BRR)

- Unit self-inspections lack commander emphasis (ADM Donald Report, CANS, CDI)

- Some nuclear related inspections have omitted areas of importance to nuclear surety (ADM Donald Report)

- Changes to Air Force policies and processes degraded the level of control for sensitive missile components (ADM Donald Report)

- Lessons-learned from the unauthorized weapons transfer were not shared in a manner to allow each of the nuclear related sites to gain an understanding of the event and determine if similar weaknesses existed at their sites (ADM Donald Report)

Action Plan

The following action plans highlight initiatives to standardize nuclear inspection processes, refine policy and guidance, restore a culture of accountability, rebuild a "zero defect" culture, and increase the nuclear focus across the Air Force.

Robust Nuclear Inspections, Staff Assistance Visits, and Unit Quality Assurance Programs

- (Doctrine, Organization) SAF/IG will 1) implement complete, independent oversight of the nuclear inspection and assessment processes, including 100% oversight of NSIs; 2) establish a centrally-managed core team of highly–experienced NSI inspectors to participate in nuclear inspections; 3) recommend procedures for reporting and adjudicating discrepancies between inspection teams and oversight authorities for consideration by the Nuclear Oversight Board (NOB); 4) establish an AF-wide inspector training and certification program; and 5) incorporate a robust no-notice program into nuclear evaluations at all CONUS units and where feasible at OCONUS units. (BRR-06; CANS-18; CDI-02; Schlesinger Report-16, -25) *Complete within 6 to 18 months, with oversight of NSIs to begin immediately* (AFI 90-201)

Note: MAJCOM/CCs will retain full NSI certification authority and retain responsibilities to conduct NORIs.

- (Doctrine, Organization) SAF/IG will lead Air Force efforts to rewrite AFI 90-201, *Inspector General Activities,* and advocate modifying T.O. 11N-25-1, *DoD Nuclear Weapons Technical Inspection System,* to improve standardization and clarify inspection guidance; to include expanding the scope of nuclear inspections, and oversight of unit quality assurance evaluators and processes. (ADM Donald Report-05; BRR-14, -22; CANS-19; Schlesinger Report-16) *Complete within 6 months* (AFI 90-201; T.O.11N-25-1)

- (Doctrine) AF/A10 (AF/A3/5N) in concert with MAJCOM commanders will promulgate policy requiring Inspector General involvement in the process of developing operational and procedural guidance for nuclear-related inspections. (Schlesinger Report-26) *Complete within 6 to 18 months* (AFI 90-201)

- (Organization, Training, Materiel) The SAF/IG and MAJCOMs will develop formal processes to impart information throughout the nuclear enterprise in order to share trend information and potential systemic issues as well as best practices. Examples include NSI Process Review Conferences, Nuclear Mission Summits, Nuclear Surety Councils, Wing Cross-talks, and information technology (IT) solutions. (BRR-06, -12; CANS-18; DSB-13) *Complete within 6 to 18 months* (AFI 90-201)

- (Organization, Training) AF/A4 will coordinate with MAJCOMs to expand quality assurance programs to comprehensively review functional areas in order to proactively detect errors and deficiencies. (ADM Donald Report-06; CANS-18) *Complete within 6 months* (AFI 21-204)

- (Doctrine, Leadership, Training) SAF/IG will institute positive measures at all levels to overhaul documentation and causal analysis, applying depth and rigor missing from current processes. Improved processes must be able to identify trends, discern systemic issues and remedy longstanding deficiencies. (ADM Donald Report-05, -06; CANS-18, -19) *Complete within 6 to 18 months* (AFI 90-201)

- (Materiel) SAF/IG will create an Air Force-wide common findings data management construct that supports automated trend analysis and regularly updates commanders to enhance identification of systemic nuclear weaknesses—e.g. Dashboard. (ADM Donald Report-04; BRR-06, -12; CANS-19; DSB-04; Schlesinger Report-16) *Complete within 6 to 18 months* (AFI 90-201)

- (Doctrine) Secretary of the Air Force's Smart Operations for the 21st Century (SAF/SO) will develop an AFI to standardize Air Force Corrective Action Processes targeted at unit-level deficiency resolution. (BRR-14; CANS-18; CDI-02) *Complete within 6 to 18 months*

Refine Policy and Guidance

- (Doctrine) AF/A10 (AF/A3/5N) will coordinate with HAF and MAJCOM team to develop a systematic process to identify nuclear-related AFIs and transform them into publications which are comprehensive and directive. (BRR-14; Aug 2008 GreyBeard Panel Report) *Complete within 12 to 18 months*

- (Doctrine) AF/A10 (AF/A3/5N) will coordinate with HAF Directorates to develop a systematic process of conducting recurring, comprehensive reviews of Air Force guidance and instructions on nuclear-related operations, maintenance, security, safety, support, and inspections to ensure currency, clarity and reduce all ambiguity. (BRR-06, -14, Schlesinger Report-03, -14, -15) *Complete within 90 days*

- (Doctrine) AFMC Sustainment Engineering and Technical Data Operations/Policy Branch (AFMC/A4YE) will establish an agile and fully resourced system for managing interim changes for nuclear-related procedures and publications. (Schlesinger Report-03, -15) *Complete within 6 months* (AFI 33-360)

- (Doctrine) SAF/IG will update inspection guidance to eliminate ambiguities with DoD guidance and standardize across MAJCOMs. SAF/IG will adjudicate all questions regarding standards and criteria as they arise and will establish procedures to adjudicate discrepancies between the AFIA and MAJCOM inspection teams. (BRR-06) *Complete within 6 to 18 months* (AFI 90-201)

- (Doctrine) MAJCOMs will standardize Nuclear Staff Assistance Visit (NSAV) and NSSAV guidance with SAF/IG and Air Force Safety (AF/SE), where applicable (e.g. tracking, trend analysis, closure). (AFNTF; DSB-04; Schlesinger Report-24, -26) *Complete within 6 to 18 months* (MAJCOM-level directives)

- (Doctrine) SAF/IG will revise applicable guidance to add inspection of nuclear weapon related materiel management and accountability during inspections. (CANS-18; CDI-02) *Complete within 6 to 18 months* (AFI 90-201)

- (Doctrine) Air Force Logistics, Installations, and Mission Support (AF/A4/7) will revise 21-, 23-, and 63- series AFIs to consolidate and standardize quality assurance guidance. (ADM Donald Report-06; CANS-19; CDI-02) *Complete within 6 to 18 months* (21-, 23-, 63- series AFIs)

- (Doctrine) SAF/IG will publish AF-level inspection/evaluation checklists across the nuclear enterprise and establish processes to maintain currency and standardization of functional inspection checklists. HAF Directorates and MAJCOMs will assist SAF/IG. (ADM Donald Report-06; AFRIT-07; CANS-18) *Complete within 6 to 18 months* (AFI 90-201; AFI 33-360)

- (Doctrine) AF/SE will review and update 91- series policy instructions to codify the culture of accountability. (Schlesinger Report-03) *Complete within 6 to 18 months* (91- series AFIs)

- (DOTMLPF) Air Force senior nuclear advocate will request the combatant commands provide clear nuclear mission requirements, to include rapid response commitment. (DSB-04; Schlesinger Report-16) *Complete within 6 months*

Restore Culture of Accountability

- (Leadership) MAJCOMs will ensure officer and NCO engagement/oversight in all nuclear enterprise activities to improve formal supervision. (AFRIT-02; BRR-13; Schlesinger Report-28, -30) *Enduring* (MAJCOM-level instructions)

- (Leadership) MAJCOMs will re-invigorate wing commander ownership of unit self-inspection programs. (ADM Donald Report-05, -06; Schlesinger Report-24, -25, -26) *Enduring* (MAJCOM-level instructions)

Restore Rigid Adherence to Standards and "Zero Defect" Culture

- (Leadership) Leadership at all levels will declare, unequivocally and frequently, that a reliable, safe, secure, and credible nuclear deterrence is a high priority and essential to national security. (BRR-13,-32; CANS-01; DSB-07, -08; Schlesinger Report-13, -14, -17) *Enduring*

- (Leadership) Commanders at all levels will establish a zero defect nuclear culture that communicates and enforces rigid adherence to standards. (Schlesinger Report-17) *Enduring*

Increase Nuclear Focus

- (Organization, Training) Air Combat Command (ACC) established, and Air Force Global Strike Command (AFGSC) will continue to refine, the implementation of a Global Deterrence Force (GDF) dedicated to supporting the USSTRATCOM mission. The GDF is a rotational approach designed to create a balance between the strategic/nuclear deterrence mission and current conventional operational requirements. The end state for the GDF is to build and sustain long term-nuclear expertise while maintaining the conventional capability to support today's fight. (Schlesinger Report-28, -30) *IOC October 2008—Enduring* (ACC directive)

- (Doctrine, Training) MAJCOMs will develop NORI scenarios that validate a unit's ability to meet rapid response commitments. (CDI-02; DSB-04; Schlesinger Report-16) *Complete within 6 to 18 months* (AFI 90-201)

- (Training, Leadership) Career Field Managers (CFMs) in coordination with Air Education and Training Command (AETC) will develop training plans to ingrain root cause analysis, self-assessment culture, and nuclear purpose values early and often (e.g. basic training, technical school, First Term Airman's Center (FTAC), Career Development Course (CDC), Nuclear Munitions Officer Course (NMOC), formal training unit (FTU), Space 100). Increase the coverage of nuclear policy, technical and operational issues at all levels of officer, enlisted and civilian professional military education. (BRR-18, -20; CANS-19; DSB-13; Schlesinger Report-25, -26) *Complete within 6 to 18 months* (AETC Instruction)

Chapter 3 — Rebuild Nuclear Expertise

> *"In no other profession are the penalties for employing untrained personnel so appalling or so irrevocable as in the military."*
>
> *General Douglas MacArthur*

Problem Statement

Air Force nuclear expertise has eroded to the point that multiple positions throughout the enterprise reflect a requirements/assignments mismatch.

Success Criteria and Desired Sub-Objectives

The Air Force is committed to revitalizing nuclear expertise at all levels. Trained and qualified personnel will demonstrate proficiency and rigid adherence to standards in the nuclear mission. The key to successfully revitalizing our nuclear expertise is a development system that matches requirements with assignments. This process will ensure the Air Force assigns the right airman, with the right skills, to the right job, while continuing to develop tomorrow's leaders.

To overcome the erosion of nuclear expertise, the Air Force examined education and training across the enterprise, improved the identification and tracking of nuclear experience and expertise, and established a force development governance construct to ensure continual, formalized senior leadership involvement in the development of future nuclear leaders.

The AF/A1, in conjunction with Air University and a panel of functional and major command representatives, reviewed the complete spectrum of officer and enlisted Professional Military Education (PME). Course modifications are underway to ensure a stair-stepped approach to Nuclear Deterrence Theory (Knowledge, Comprehension, and Application) across the continuum of education from basic to senior developmental education. The full scope of formal training courses, some taught within the Air Education and Training Command (AETC) structure and some outside, was also reviewed by the expert panel. Additional nuclear content is necessary in the curriculum of some advanced courses. New courses are required for nuclear leadership roles and institutional rigor (standards of learning and formalized objectives) are necessary in courses outside the AETC classroom. Inspection and evaluation criteria are being developed by Air Force training experts for non-AETC courses to ensure consistency and adherence to training objectives.

Key nuclear billets have been formally identified and Special Experience Identifiers (SEIs) developed and assigned to ensure individuals filling key positions possess the required background and experiences to effectively lead the nuclear enterprise. Identifying key billets outside of standard AF organizations (e.g., Dept of Energy,

Defense Threat Reduction Agency, etc.) will broaden the expertise and experience of Air Force nuclear leaders.

Finally, senior leadership involvement in developing nuclear leaders will be institutionalized through the Nuclear Enterprise Advisory Panel (NEAP). The NEAP, chaired by the new AF/A10 (AF/A3/5N), serves as a cross functional review and advisory panel to the FMDC, chaired by the Vice Chief of Staff of the Air Force. The NEAP will provide force development oversight for officers, enlisted, and civilian personnel — those within purely nuclear career fields and those in supporting, and equally important, roles.

The combination of these efforts addressing education and training, identifying and tracking nuclear expertise, and formal senior leadership oversight of nuclear force development is designed to reverse the erosion of nuclear skills and expertise within the Air Force. More work remains to be done, but the Air Force has already begun moving forward and shown commitment to rebuilding expertise in the nuclear enterprise.

Root Causes

Detailed analysis revealed common root cause categories: 1) reduced priority of the nuclear mission, contributing to 2) reduced focus on development and management of nuclear subject matter experts; both of which culminate in 3) inadequate education and training programs or guidance for personnel in some areas of the nuclear mission. In addition, concerns arose over the quantity of nuclear experts, depth of the nuclear expertise, and quality of Air Force processes for building expertise.

Reduced Priority of the Nuclear Mission

- Nuclear-related aviator experience and expertise is diminishing within the bomber and DCA units (BRR)

- Nuclear exercises are not meeting current requirements in frequency or scale (BRR, DSB)

- Focus on nuclear training has shifted as a result of the increased COCOM requirements for conventional force capabilities (BRR)

Reduced Focus on Development and Management of Nuclear Subject Matter Experts

- Insufficient manning has been provided to nuclear commanders to execute their missions and manpower authorizations supporting the nuclear mission have decreased below long-term sustainment levels (Schlesinger Report)

- The diminishing base of nuclear experience in some support specialties makes it difficult to select and prepare leaders for command and supervisory positions (BRR)

- The lack of understanding as to which manpower authorizations are vital to the nuclear mission has resulted in the deployment of key nuclear personnel elsewhere and the inability to determine which critical billets require special management (Schlesinger Report)

- Air Force leadership needs to develop a more effective approach to personnel management for manning critical nuclear positions (Schlesinger Report)

- Current management of nuclear-related career fields is not adequate without a complementary program to support the development of people within the nuclear community (Schlesinger Report)

- The Air Force needs to increase opportunities for presence and influence in key nuclear billets, especially in joint and interagency organizations, by filling these positions with highly-qualified individuals (BRR)

- Nuclear sustainment manpower is inconsistent with today's mission requirements (CANS)

- Leadership in the Air Force's nuclear enterprise is professional and dedicated, but experience levels continue to decline (BRR)

- The Air Force is not consistently leveraging educational opportunities to optimize follow-on assignments or presence in key nuclear billets (BRR)

- There is no deliberate force development and retention management for the nuclear sustainment enterprise workforce (CANS)

Inadequate Education and Training Programs or Guidance
- The nuclear force requires clear and detailed direction in instructions and technical orders particularly in light of a less-experienced workforce, especially in aircraft units (BRR)

- Accountability of nuclear weapons in the Air Force is sound; however, additional experience and training for Munitions Accountable Systems Officers (MASOs) will enhance the current process, particularly on the Defense Integration and Management of Nuclear Data Services system (DIAMONDS) (BRR)

- Major commands and Numbered Air Forces have created specific nuclear training programs that are external to the formal and institutionalized training curriculum oversight (BRR)

- The curricula of professional military education schools and courses devote at best only minimal time and attention to nuclear-related topics (BRR)

- The curricula of resident and nonresident professional military education (PME) for officers and enlisted personnel turns up only a very small number of nuclear-related topics (Schlesinger Report)

- Training in nuclear operations—for example, the Strategic Weapons School—was streamlined to the point of elimination (Schlesinger Report)

- Training required within the nuclear sustainment enterprise is inadequate (CANS)

Action Plan

Rebuilding nuclear expertise in the Air Force will require senior leadership involvement in requirements determination and prioritization, personnel and development processes, and realistic education, training, and exercise participation.

- (Personnel) AF/A1 will review nuclear manpower standards to ensure all nuclear workload is captured. (AFRIT-08, -09; BRR-33, -34; CANS-05; CDI-10; Schlesinger Report-21, -29, -34, -35) *Complete within 6 to 18 months* (AFI 38-201)

- (Personnel) AF/A1 will assess nuclear mission career fields to ensure program budget decision reductions were appropriately targeted and left no seams in enterprise support. (BRR-04, -34) *Complete within 6 months* (AFI 38-201; AFI 38-204)

- (Personnel) AF/A1 will review medical manpower requirements at installations with large Personnel Reliability Program (PRP) populations to ensure adequate documentation and resourcing of manpower requirements. (BRR-33) *Complete within 6 months* (AFI 41-210; AFI 38-201)

- (Personnel) AF/A1 will review logistics composite models (LCOM) to determine if they provide enough manpower for dual-tasked and prime nuclear airlift force (PNAF) units to meet mission requirements. (AFRIT-09; BRR-33; CANS-05) *Complete within 6 to 18 months* (AFI 38-201)

- (Personnel) AF/A1 will review existing manpower (non-LCOM) determinant products to determine if dual-tasked and PNAF workloads are adequately reflected in each product. (AFRIT-09; BRR-33; CANS-05) *Complete within 6 months* (AFI 38-201)

Air Force Senior Leader Oversight of Air Force Nuclear Enterprise Personnel Development

Senior leader involvement is imperative to ensure that the personnel planning and development processes support the needs of the nuclear enterprise. Leaders must ensure that processes are in-place and followed for requirement identification, development, and tracking to support a highly reliable nuclear enterprise end state. The

NEAP will institutionalize this process serving as the nuclear cross functional review under the Vice Chief of Staff of the Air Force's FMDC.

- (Doctrine, Organization, Leadership) The FMDC will charter a NEAP to improve oversight of the management and development of personnel for the nuclear enterprise. Because the nuclear enterprise is manned by personnel from many career fields, membership in the NEAP will be broad. The NEAP will be chaired by the new AF/A10 and will provide regular updates to the FMDC. The NEAP generally will be responsible for detailing personnel management and/or development requirements and for providing similar personnel oversight for the nuclear mission area as a career field manager would provide to a career field. (AFRIT-08; BRR-18, -20; CANS-04; Schlesinger Report-18, -29, -31) *The NEAP charter, and its relationship to the overall FMDC construct will be drafted and staffed within 30 days* (AFI 36-2640; NEAP Charter)

Robust Management of Nuclear Subject Matter Experts

Air Force senior leaders remain critical in developing the actionable steps for resolving the erosion of nuclear enterprise expertise. AF/A10 (A3/5N), with support from AF/A1, HAF functional authorities, and MAJCOM commanders and their staffs, will provide an actionable plan to ensure the Air Force develops nuclear expertise. Already, AF/A1 has led efforts, in coordination with MAJCOMs and Functional Managers, to identify key nuclear billets, and has identified and assigned Special Experience Identifiers (SEIs) to ensure individuals filling key positions possess the required background and experiences to effectively lead the nuclear enterprise. Further work remains. Emphasis will be placed on six strategic processes:

- (Personnel) AF/A1 will develop a comprehensive list of all key nuclear-related positions in the nuclear enterprise and ensure they receive priority for assigning experienced personnel. (AFRIT-09; BRR-33; Schlesinger Report-34, -35) *Complete within 6 months (AFI 38-201)*

- (Doctrine, Training, Personnel) Once the nuclear key billets are identified, the NEAP will coordinate with MAJCOMs and COCOMs to define the training, education, and experiential requirements for key positions within the nuclear enterprise. (AFRIT-08; BRR-07, -18, -20; CANS-04; Schlesinger Report-05, -29) *Complete within 6 to 18 months (AFI 36-2302)*

- (Doctrine, Personnel) The NEAP will work with Air Force Functional Managers to formalize a career development plan for officers, enlisted, and civilians. These plans will define the depth and breadth of experience necessary for them to assume leadership positions in the nuclear enterprise. (BRR-01, -03, -04, -18; Schlesinger Report-18) *Complete within 6 months (AFI 36-2640)*

- (Doctrine, Personnel) AF/A1, in coordination with the NEAP, will ensure officer and enlisted nuclear career fields are viable and adequately manned (AFRIT-09; BRR-01, -04, -33; CANS-04; CDI-01, -02, -10; Schlesinger Report-05, -34, -35). *Complete within 6 months*

- (Doctrine, Materiel, Personnel) AF/A1 will develop a reliable and easily accessible system to track nuclear experience across the entire Air Force. (BRR-01, -04) *Complete within 6 to 18 months* (Airman Capability Management initiative guidance (to be developed following pilot effort))

- (Doctrine, Personnel) The NEAP will work with Air Force Functional Managers and AF/A1 to ensure appropriate career broadening opportunities (such as maintenance, system engineering, program management, and policy related assignments) are in place to develop officers for leadership roles in nuclear enterprise. (BRR-01) *Complete within 6 to 18 months* (AFI 36-2640)

The nuclear personnel development process must be part of the larger, integrated Air Force leadership development process. Recapturing nuclear mission excellence is the Air Force's top priority and demands a collective effort, balanced across the institution, to ensure excellence in every mission discipline.

Improve Education and Training Programs and Guidance

Realistic training and exercise participation is required at all levels of the enterprise to hone operational expertise. The Air Force must invest time and resources to refine nuclear proficiency. Realistic training and exercises provide opportunities to cement sound standards of behavior and create a feedback mechanism for developing consistent duty performance. The AF/A1 led a team to review the complete spectrum of officer and enlisted PME. Course modifications are underway. Formal training courses were also reviewed. As a result, additional nuclear content is necessary in the curriculum of some advanced courses. New courses are required for nuclear leadership roles and institutional rigor (standards of learning and formalized objectives) are necessary in courses outside the AETC classroom. Inspection and evaluation criteria are being developed by Air Force training experts for non-AETC courses to ensure consistency and adherence to training objectives. The Air Force will take the following actions to restore rigor to nuclear operations, exercises, and inspections, with lessons learned/conclusions shared across the Air Force:

- (Training, Leadership) AF/A1 facilitated an initial joint training and education review on 3-4 Sep 08 with nuclear enterprise career field managers to establish nuclear training and education baselines and determine if current training and education portfolios are sufficient. The results were reviewed by curriculum development experts at Air University and proposed curriculum modifications have been forwarded to the Air Force Learning Committee, a subordinate panel to the FMDC, for validation and approval. (AFRIT-08; BRR-18, -20; CANS-04; Schlesinger Report-11, -29) *Complete within 6 months* (AFI 36-2201; AFLC CONOPS; IDE/SDE CONOPS; AFI 36-2301)

- (Training, Leadership) Air University (AU) will develop a short course at Maxwell Air Force Base (AFB) for new commanders to address nuclear doctrine, procedures, and operational arts to include instruction on accountability and custody. (BRR-04) *This item is complete* (AFI 36-2302)

- (Training, Leadership) AF/A1, in conjunction with functional managers and appropriate MAJCOMs, will identify key billets in the nuclear enterprise to be filled with graduates of the National Laboratory Technical Fellowship Program (NLTFP) and/or Air Force Institute of Technology nuclear engineer program graduates. (BRR-21) *Complete within 6 months* (IDE/SDE CONOPS; AFI 36-2301; AFI 36-2302)

- (Training) MAJCOMs will utilize focused nuclear-related leadership training for Airmen prior to assuming command or supervisory roles in the nuclear enterprise. (BRR-04; CDI-03, -05) *Complete within 6 months (*MAJCOM-level directives)

- (Training, Leadership) MAJCOM commanders will ensure unit mission and quality assurance training is sufficient to meet mission needs and their staffs will certify results to the NEAP. (CDI-01, -02, -06) *Complete within 6 months*

- (Training, Leadership) AF/A10 (AF/A3/5N), in coordination with MAJCOMs and COCOMs, will review/validate frequency, scale, of nuclear exercises. NORIs will execute to the DOC statement. AF/CV will be waiver approval authority for movement/cancellation of scheduled nuclear exercises. (BRR-13, Schlesinger Report-16) *Complete within 6 months*

- (Doctrine, Training) SAF/IG will develop a standardized training, qualification, and certification program for all members of IG teams that conduct nuclear inspections. (BRR-06, -12; CANS-18; Schlesinger Report-16, -25, -26) *Complete within 6 to 18 months*

The combination of these efforts addressing requirements, education and training, identifying and tracking nuclear expertise, and formal senior leadership oversight of nuclear force development is designed to reverse the erosion of nuclear skills and expertise within the Air Force.

Chapter 4 — Sustainment

> *"I don't ever, ever, ever want to hear the term logistics tail again. If our aircraft, missiles, and weapons are the teeth of our military might, then logistics is the muscle, tendons, and sinews that make the teeth bite down and hold on—logistics is the jawbone! Hear that? The JAWBONE!"*
>
> *Lt Gen Leo Marquez, USAF*

Problem Statement

The Air Force lacks an end-to-end systems approach to nuclear life-cycle sustainment.

Success Criteria and Desired Sub-Objectives

The Air Force must organize the nuclear sustainment enterprise with clear lines of authority and responsibility, comprehensive logistics and supply chain management, sound maintenance, inventory, and distribution processes, responsive engineering support, and robust and comprehensive training at all levels. Desired sub-objectives include:

- The Air Force must reverse the dispersion of nuclear expertise and sustainment capability by reestablishing a clear and focused organizational architecture, consolidate and clarify responsibility and authority, and eliminate inter-organizational confusion (Organizational change attributes are incorporated into Chapter 7)

- The Air Force must positively control nuclear weapons-related materiel (NWRM) separate from normal supply chain items. Directives must be thoroughly reviewed to eliminate inaccuracies, inconsistencies, and confusion. New directives pertaining directly to NWRM processes and management must be written

- Units responsible for handling NWRM must be appropriately equipped with personnel, tools, infrastructure, and guidance to establish and maintain a streamlined, auditable, and standardized positive inventory control (PIC) system for all such materiel

- Engineering support throughout the Air Force nuclear enterprise must be 1) documented; 2) attributable; and 3) authored by a cognizant engineering authority

- The Air Force must institute robust and comprehensive training programs for nuclear sustainment at all levels, including oversight and assessment (Overall training and expertise is addressed in Chapter 3)

Root Causes

The AFNTF identified the following areas as root causes of issues within the nuclear sustainment enterprise.

Lack of Critical Self-Assessment

- Oversight, inspection, and internal audits have been ineffective in resolving recurring deficiencies (ADM Donald Report, BRR, DSB)

- The ICBM communities, including maintenance, engineering, operations, and logistic organizations, have a poorly developed self-assessment culture (ADM Donald Report, DSB)

- The Air Force failed to implement methodologies and processes for identifying systemic weaknesses and root causes (ADM Donald Report, BRR, CANS)

Inadequate Guidance

- The Air Force has not sufficiently defined nor provided governing policy for managing NWRM (ADM Donald Report, AFRIT, CANS)

- Deficient supply chain processes and noncompliance with related procedures degraded control of sensitive missile components (ADM Donald Report)

- The informal process for engineering support delays responsiveness, hinders trend analysis, and introduces unnecessary technical and programmatic risk (ADM Donald Report, CANS)

- Logistics and supply chain management policies, procedures, and processes across the Air Force nuclear enterprise are not clear, concise, nor standardized (ADM Donald Report, CANS)

- The current Air Force supply chain does not effectively manage or positively control NWRM (ADM Donald Report, AFRIT, CANS)

- Nuclear policy, procedures, and processes affecting wing sustainment operations are confusing and non-standard (ADM Donald Report, CANS)

- Policies for DULL SWORD nuclear reporting are not clear, resulting in inconsistent or random reporting (CANS)

- There are systemic breakdowns in the technical order sustainment process (CANS)

- Shortcomings exist in the training for Munitions Accountable Systems Officers (MASO), particularly on the Defense Integration and Management of Nuclear Data Services system (AFRIT, BRR, CANS)

- Air Force oversight and assessment processes for nuclear sustainment activities to include inspections, Logistics Standardization and Evaluation Team (LSET)/Maintenance Standardization and Evaluation Team (MSET), and self-inspections are non-standard across the nuclear sustainment enterprise (BRR, CANS)

- Changes to Air Force policies and processes degraded the level of control for sensitive missile components (ADM Donald Report, CANS)

- Multiple independent data/messaging systems cause confusion, and consume time and resources (CANS)

- Air Force documentation was inadequate to demonstrate that current personnel and area radiation exposure and monitoring practices are sufficient to ensure exposure is less than Air Force requirements and maintained as low as reasonably achievable. No evidence of recent oversight of this program by authorities, either external or internal, was found (ADM Donald Report)

Lack of Sustainment Advocacy

- Dispersed authority and responsibility have created an environment ill-suited for setting and maintaining standards necessary for nuclear weapons (ADM Donald Report, BRR, DSB)

- The ICBM engineering community lacks a clear major command owner and has deteriorated in the exercise of technical authority (ADM Donald Report, CANS)

- There is no single funding advocate for the Air Force nuclear sustainment enterprise (BRR, CANS)

- Leadership does not adequately oversee nor review nuclear sustainment areas (ADM Donald Report, BRR, CANS)

Action Plan

Given the unequivocal need for positive control, redundancy, and reliability, achieving efficiencies within the Air Force nuclear enterprise is not always desirable or attainable.

- (DOTMLPF) AF/A10 (AF/A3/5N) will coordinate with HAF and MAJCOMs to refine the definition of the Air Force nuclear enterprise sufficiently to identify and execute all respective activities. (AFNTF; August 2008 GreyBeard Panel Report) *Complete within 6 months*

Establish a Functional Organizational Structure with Clear Lines of Authority and Responsibility

See Chapter 7.

Develop Comprehensive Logistics and Supply Chain Management Processes

- (DOTMLPF) AF/A4/7 and the Air Force Nuclear Weapons Center (AFNWC) will continue the process of identifying, physically marking, controlling, and overseeing NWRM to achieve PIC for these assets. The AFNWC PIC facility will store all NWRM inventory that is not authorized to support base required inventory levels. They will also oversee inventory that is in transit, depot repair, and contract repair. A group of dedicated, nuclear-trained professionals assigned to the AFNWC will manage, control and store this NWRM. PIC for these and other critical assets require a phased approach that will initially be manually intensive until processes are automated and transitioned to the new logistics electronic records program solution, the Expeditionary Combat Support System (ECSS). Specific responsibilities for the AFNWC are outlined in AFMC Mission Directive 421, *Air Force Nuclear Weapons Center.* (ADM Donald Report-01, -02, -03, -07; AFRIT-01, -03, -04, -05, -06; CANS-10, -11, -12; Schlesinger Report-15) *Complete within 6 months* (AFMAN 23-110; AFI 21-203)

  Phase I: Gain immediate PIC of the National Stock Numbers (NSNs) identified by the AF and OSD as NWRM by transferring these assets from Defense Logistics Agency (DLA) into Air Force owned and managed facilities. Completing this phase will require Air Force Materiel Command (AFMC) to develop a programming plan (P-Plan) that addresses the following:

    o Warehouse facility and security upgrades

    o Warehouse IT and item identification systems

    o Warehouse manning

    o Training

    o Policy and procedures

    o On-base transportation capability

    o Dedicated distribution network

  Re-warehousing these assets under Air Force control will eliminate excess "handoffs" between the Air Force and DLA. The Air Force is developing a concept of operations (CONOPS) including people, processes and systems to provide PIC for these assets. Where current system capability will not provide the automated level of in-transit and serial number tracking needed, the Air Force will assign additional manpower to provide aggressive manual tracking as required. An interim IT solution is projected for December 2008 to automate some manual management tasks.

Phase II: Expand PIC to include additional nuclear-related materiel not identified as NWRM (as required). Expand IT solution capability to incorporate increased automated capability.

Phase III: Enable ECSS to provide the real-time visibility and serial number tracking needed to establish fully automated positive inventory control. Full operational capability (FOC) is currently scheduled for 2013.

- (Personnel) AF/A4/7 will differentiate assigned Logistics Readiness Squadron personnel to distinguish those directly involved with NWRM and additional nuclear-related materiel not identified as NWRM from inventory managers. (Schlesinger Report-15) *Complete within 6 to 18 months* (Enlisted Classification Directory)

- (Doctrine) The Nuclear Weapons System Safety Group (NWSSG) will review the NWRM list and identify any changes to the critical component list. (AFRIT-03; CANS-10) *Complete within 6 to 18 months* (Master Nuclear Certification List)

- (Doctrine) AF/A4/7 will schedule and assign systematic assessments and updates of all required publications, directives, and technical orders to correct errors, clarify/deconflict guidance, and reinvigorate assessment processes. This review will be separate from other reviews and applied specifically to supply chain management. (AFRIT-07; BRR-22; CANS-11, -12; Schlesinger Report-15) *Complete within 18 months* (AFMAN 23-110; AFPD 23-1; AFI 21-203)

- (Doctrine, Materiel) AFMC will verify excess backlog and create a 5-year disposition plan for NWRM service spares items no longer required. (AFRIT-11; CANS-12) *Complete within 18 months* (AFMAN 23-110; AFI 21-203)

Refine Maintenance, Inventory, and Distribution Processes

- (Materiel, Facilities) AF/A4/7 will assess current and future nuclear maintenance concepts to determine if nuclear-related facilities and equipment meet nuclear sustainment requirements while solving Air Force-wide deficiencies. (CANS-15; Schlesinger Report-23) *Complete within 6 to 18 months*

- (Doctrine) AFMC will develop new and revise existing technical order(s) for NWRM storage and handling with emphasis on thorough documentation, inventory management, and traceability. (AFRIT-07; BRR-22; CANS-11, -12; Schlesinger Report-15) *Complete within 6 to 18 months* (T.O. 00-20-3 and new T.O. for field level PIC use; all applicable NWRM item technical orders that currently exist)

- (Doctrine, Facilities) AF/A4/7 will evaluate the benefit of consolidating munitions and missile maintenance requirements into a single 21-200 series instruction and provide a recommendation to Air Force leadership for consideration. (CANS-16; Schlesinger Report-15) *Complete within 18 months*

- (Materiel) Commanders of nuclear units must ensure personnel who require access to nuclear weapons, have adequate availability to common communication modes (Defense Message System (DMS), Secure Internet Protocol Router Network (SIPRNet)). (CANS-15, -16) *Complete within 18 months* (AFI 21-204)

- To mitigate non-standard scheduling and tracking, the ICBM community is transitioning from the Improved Maintenance Management Program (IMMP) to the Integrated Maintenance Data System (IMDS). This usage of IMDS is an interim solution until ECSS is fielded in 2013. (BRR-27; CANS-12, -14, -16; CDI-03, -05):

  - (Doctrine, Materiel) AF/A4/7 will mandate the use of a single approved software application in Munitions Control Elements for required asset tracking/visual aid purposes. *Complete within 6 months* (AFI 21-204)

  - (Doctrine, Materiel) Electronic Systems Center (ESC) will develop a solution for shortfalls with IMDS in associating missiles to launcher/pylons. *Complete within 18 months*

  - (Doctrine) AF/A4/7 will mandate IMDS use for re-entry system mate, de-mate and handling operations. *Complete within 6 months* (AFI 21-202)

  - (Leadership) Commanders at all levels will enforce IMDS use for weapons maintenance activities. *Complete within 18 months*

- (Doctrine, Materiel) ESC will replace IMMP with IMDS. (BRR-26; CANS-14) *Complete within 18 months* (AFI 21-202; AFSPCI 21-202 VI)

- (Materiel) AFNWC will accelerate Re-entry System Test Set (RSTS) replacement to mitigate capability loss prior to initial operational capability (IOC). (CANS-15) *Complete within 18 months*

- (Doctrine) AF/A4/7 will schedule and assign systematic assessments and updates of all required publications, directives, and technical orders to correct errors, clarify/deconflict guidance, and reinvigorate assessment processes. This review will be separate from other reviews and applied specifically to maintenance, inventory and distribution processes. (AFRIT-07; BRR-22; CANS-13; DSB-02,-03; Schlesinger Report-15) *Complete within 18 months* (AFPD 21-101)

- (Doctrine, Materiel, Facilities) AF/A4/7 and AFNWC assess and implement weapons storage area (WSA) portal monitoring and move right tracking. (BRR-26) *Complete within 6 to 18 months* (AFMAN 31-108)

Improve Weapons Maintenance and Storage Safety

- (Doctrine) Air Force Safety (AF/SE) will update and standardize the intrinsic radiation (INRAD) program guidance in AFI 91-108. (ADM Donald Report; Schlesinger Report-15) *Complete within 6 months* (AFI 91-108)

- (Doctrine, Training) Air Force Surgeon General (AF/SG) as lead, with AF/SE and Air Force Inspection Agency (AFIA), will develop an INRAD Safety Inspection Checklist and evaluate requirements, training practices, and assessment of intrinsic radiation monitoring programs to ensure that exposure levels are tracked and are as low as reasonably achievable. (ADM Donald Report; Schlesinger Report-15) *Complete within 6 to 18 months*

Build Responsive Engineering Support

- (Doctrine, Leadership) AFMC will enforce use of written communication for engineering assistance and limit approval of engineering direction to the cognizant engineering authority. (ADM Donald Report-04; CANS-02) *Complete within 6 to 18 months* (T.O. 00-25-107)

- (Doctrine, Organization) AFMC and the AFNWC will develop formal processes for the engineering community that focus on technical assistance, trend analysis, and Operational Safety, Suitability and Effectiveness. (ADM Donald Report-04; CANS-06) *Complete within 6 to 18 months* (T.O. 00-25-107)

- (Doctrine, Materiel) AFMC will implement Product Lifecycle Management (PLM) capabilities to support ICBM engineering and sustainment. PLM will become the automated tool for Electronic Technical Assistance Requests (ETARS) to include appropriate direction to submit and process DULL SWORD reports as required. (CANS-02, -06; Schlesinger Report-15) *Complete within 6 to 18 months* (T.O. 00-25-107; AFMAN 91-221)

- (Doctrine, Training, Leadership) AF/SE update Air Force Manual (AFMAN) 91-221 and AFI 21-101 to direct use of Air Force Safety Automated System for DULL SWORD reporting and provide guidance for units conducting maintenance on aircraft, major subsystems, support equipment, or software involving nuclear certified equipment. (BRR-17; CANS-08) *Complete within 6 to 18 months* (AFMAN 91-221; AFI 21-101)

Bolster Training and Standardization at All Levels

- (Doctrine, Training) MAJCOMs will assess and establish a training architecture across the sustainment enterprise and revise policy to make specific training mandatory. Modify training programs to accommodate item managers, depot maintainers, transportation experts, warehousing personnel and unit-level munitions, missile, and materiel managers to ensure they are familiar with implementation, system requirements and procedures. (AFRIT-08; CANS-17) *Complete within 6 to 18 months*

- (Training) AF/A4/7 will develop/expand training requirements and courses for item managers, equipment account custodians as well as MASOs and nuclear accountability personnel. (AFRIT-02, -08; BRR-17; CANS-17) *Complete within 6 to 18 months* (AFI 21-204; AFMAN 23-110; CFETP; AFI 21-203; new AFI covering Nuclear Accountability to include weapons and NWRM)

- (Doctrine, Training, Materiel, Facilities) MAJCOMs will identify and procure trainers and equipment and develop facilities and lesson plans as necessary to ensure a robust and realistic training environment, (i.e., Realistic Weapon Trainer, Rotary Launcher, Defense Integration and Management of Nuclear Data Services (DIAMONDS) laptop, and facility requirements). (BRR-35; CANS-15; Schlesinger Report-22)

Chapter 5 — Investment: Requirements, Acquisition, and Programming

> *The expenses required to prevent a war are much lighter than those that will, if not prevented, be absolutely necessary to maintain it.*
>
> Benjamin Franklin

Problem Statement

The Air Force has underinvested in the nuclear deterrence mission and has no clear, long-term commitment to recapitalize, refresh or replace current nuclear capability.

Success Criteria and Desired Sub-Objectives

The Air Force must invest in the nuclear deterrence mission and have a clear, long-term commitment to sustain, modernize, and recapitalize its nuclear capability.

Based upon national guidance and vetted COCOM and MAJCOM requirements, the Air Force Corporate Structure (AFCS) process will provide the proper balance of capability and risk to senior leadership so that funding decisions are based upon relevant, accurate, consistent, defendable, repeatable, and transparent data and analysis, and are made with full understanding of the implications to the Air Force nuclear enterprise. The Air Force nuclear enterprise must be clearly defined with respect to the AFCS. Requirements, acquisition, programming, and programmed budget funding processes must be aligned to provide transparency into the risk, resourcing, and funding execution of all Air Force nuclear enterprise elements.

To ensure appropriate, sustained institutional commitment to the Air Force nuclear enterprise and Air Force nuclear-related capability, mid- and long-range planning and programming strategies must be refined.

AF/A8, with advocated inputs from appropriate MAJCOMs and Air Force Council deliberation, will create strategic plans that address Air Force mid-term requirements (i.e., F-35 dual capability, tanker replacement, WSA alignment, and personnel), and long-term requirements and acquisition strategies to ensure future viability of our nuclear deterrent forces (i.e., ALCM, bomber, and ICBM replacements).

AF/A8 will refine the headquarters Air Force corporate process by assigning AF/A10 (AF/A3/5N) to the Air Force Group and Board. In addition, AF/A8 will continue the evaluation of the portfolios of the existing 12 panels of the AFCS to identify Program Elements (PE) which directly or indirectly impact and comprise the Air Force nuclear enterprise; continue the evaluation of consolidating all nuclear-related PEs into one panel, or a similarly robust management portfolio; and evaluate a "beta-test" Virtual Major Force Program (vMFP) dedicated to the Air Force nuclear enterprise in order to consolidate all nuclear-related programs into one robust management and data repository.

Root Causes

End of the Cold War – De-emphasis of the Nuclear Mission

Our nation's emphasis on the nuclear enterprise and mission has eroded since the end of the Cold War. This erosion links the demise of the former Soviet Union and the change in perception of the nuclear mission and threat. The nuclear mission shifted from a national, strategic, and operational imperative of large numbers of on-alert nuclear forces, to a significantly reduced nuclear force and posture. This shift further solidified as a result of the 11 September 2001 terrorist attacks and the force protection-focused realization that terrorists might possibly target nuclear storage and operations facilities. Absent the perceived urgent need for an immediate massive nuclear response against a nuclear peer, the main focus of the nuclear mission shifted to providing strategic deterrence options and actively pursuing risk avoidance through nuclear surety and systems reliability. This new strategic environment facilitated a changed resource requirement and management mentality at COCOM and MAJCOM levels wherein sustainment and modernization programs for nuclear missions were supported and maintained, but recapitalization and investment in next generation systems, technology upgrades, or a future industrial base were identified but not made a budget priority. Coincidentally, the nation (and the Air Force) has, since August of 1990, been engaged in continuous conventional combat operations. As such, the resultant strategic and operational shift in priorities directly influenced COCOM and MAJCOM requirements *from* maintaining a robust Air Force nuclear enterprise, *to* an investment strategy more heavily focused on conventional Air Force capabilities supporting current operations. Further complicating the nuclear mission equation was the focus of both the American public and elected officials to capture a "peace dividend" in response to the end of the "Cold War." Operations tempo and personnel tempo increased substantially over the past two decades, further stressing DoD budgets, and shifted DoD-wide focus from recapitalization of aging weapon systems to funding and sustaining current operations. Findings include:

- Focus on the nuclear mission, especially in dual-capable bomber units, has diminished from the robust nuclear culture that existed during the Cold War (BRR, DSB, Schlesinger Report)

- The level of focus within major headquarters from Joint Staff to Air Force major commands was drastically reduced with little apparent consideration or understanding of the impact of such reductions across virtually all such headquarters (DSB, Schlesinger Report)

- The conventional roles of the B-52 force so dominate the nuclear role that there is minimum daily attention to the nuclear role outside the restricted area where nuclear weapons are stored and maintained. Moving nuclear weapons from where the majority of B-52 strategic bombers are based is likely to further complicate focus on the nuclear mission and further devalue the nuclear mission (DSB, Schlesinger Report)

No Single Advocate for Requirements, Acquisition, and Programming for Air Force Nuclear Enterprise Funding

Nuclear mission requirements span a wide spectrum of organizations to include COCOMs and MAJCOMs. Air Force requirements, acquisition and programming processes lack a single entity focused on Air Force nuclear capabilities. Diffusion of responsibility for resourcing across several entities has resulted in nuclear-related requirements, acquisition and programming initiatives not receiving a focused review within the AFCS process.

Nuclear mission requirements span a wide spectrum of organizations to include COCOMs and MAJCOMs. Air Force requirements, acquisition and programming processes lack a single entity focused on Air Force nuclear capabilities. Diffusion of responsibility for resourcing across several entities has resulted in nuclear-related Requirements, Acquisition and Programming initiatives not receiving a focused review within the AFCS process.

- No comprehensive process exists to ensure sustained investment advocacy (Schlesinger Report)

- When reorganized in the 1990s, the Air Force dispersed command authority and responsibility for the nuclear mission. This left no central advocate, undercut mission alignment with its primary customer, and blurred lines of authority (Schlesinger Report)

- There is no single funding advocate for sustainment of the Air Force nuclear enterprise (CANS)

- Current Air Force nuclear organizational construct fragments nuclear weapons advocacy and policy (BRR)

- To improve upon missile field security, there is a critical need to fully fund a replacement helicopter and to fund the sustainment costs of the remote visual assessment (BRR)

- Funding for second destination transportation to move nuclear weapons is inadequate (BRR)

Air Force Requirements, Acquisition, and Programming Processes must Enhance Capabilities and Define Risk to the Air Force Nuclear Enterprise

In addition to the conscious national-level decision to reduce nuclear force structure, the Air Force has balanced nuclear sustainment and life cycle management via corporate decisions in Program Objective Memorandum (POM) exercises since the 1990s. The AFCS is designed to bring together cross-functional issues, however, the process is not optimized to segregate, or identify connections to portions of program elements which may have first, second, or third order effects on the Air Force nuclear enterprise, its operations, sustainment, or other elements of the nuclear mission. This overall challenge is further complicated by the fact that the term "Air Force nuclear enterprise" was neither previously defined, nor refined for the AFCS.

- Aging transportation and handling equipment is adding to the stress on units with a nuclear mission (BRR)

- Systems and equipment supporting the nuclear mission are aging and continue to impact reliability and availability (BRR)

Disconnects Between Final Budget and Execution in the Air Force Nuclear Enterprise

In a post-POM environment after Congress passes the budget and the President signs it, Air Force leaders continue to be faced with evolving and increasing real-time operational needs that must be addressed. This changing environment sometimes results in a diversion of funds from specific program areas designated in the POM to other programs during "current year" execution to meet these urgent priorities. This critical tool allows, and must continue to allow, commanders to respond to changing environments that may be driven by existing time delays from programming to actual expenditure of funds; however, there may be unintended consequences to the Air Force nuclear enterprise as a result of these actions.

- Budget execution may have caused resource allocation weaknesses in field support for the nuclear mission (BRR, Schlesinger Report)

Dedicated, focused, and more robust advocacy will help the requirements, acquisition, and programming processes ensure the Air Force can adequately sustain, modernize, and recapitalize the Air Force nuclear enterprise.

Action Plan

Re-emphasize the Nuclear Mission

In accordance with the Air Force number one priority to revitalize the Air Force nuclear enterprise, the Annual Planning and Programming Guidance (APPG) will reflect minimal risk to the Air Force nuclear enterprise during the POM process. This clear statement of the level of minimal risk to the Air Force nuclear enterprise in the APPG will further bolster the efforts of a single nuclear advocate during requirements, acquisition, and programming process deliberations.

- (DOTMLPF) AF/A10 (AF/A3/5N) will clearly refine the definition of the Air Force nuclear enterprise with respect to AFCS processes. (ADM Donald Report-02, -07; BRR-08; DSB-02, -03, -07, -12; Schlesinger Report-32) *Complete in less than 6 months* (AFI 16-501)

Programs which are DX-rated indicate the highest national defense priority within the Defense Priorities and Allocation System (DPAS). Minuteman III, Air Launched Cruise

Missiles (ALCM), and B-2 Aircraft Programs have historically been rated as DX programs. In 2006, Office of the Secretary of Defense, Acquisition, Technology, and Logistics (OSD/AT&L) removed the DX rating from all Air Force nuclear programs, de-emphasizing the importance of the Air Force nuclear mission and holding future delivery schedules and sustainment efforts at risk due to the lower DPAS rating competing in a common supplier base. The Navy Trident D-5 Program remains a DX-rated program, emphasizing the high priority placed on the US Navy's nuclear mission. The US Air Force needs long-term commitment, resources, and robust advocacy from national leadership, DoD, and other agencies to sustain, recapitalize, replace, and/or refresh nuclear capability and personnel in-accordance-with the recommendations made in the Air Force nuclear enterprise roadmap.

- (Doctrine) Under Secretary of the Air Force (SAF/US) and Assistant Secretary of the Air Force Acquisition (SAF/AQ) will request Office Secretary of Defense, Acquisition, Technology, and Logistics (OSD/AT&L) reinstate the DX rating for Air Force nuclear systems and programs (in line with those of the US Navy). (BRR-07) *Complete within 6 months (Memorandum from SecAF requesting nomination for DX status will be submitted to the DUSD(IP) IAW DoD 4400.1-M "Department of Defense Priorities and Allocations Manual")*

Single Advocate for Requirements, Acquisition, and Programming for Air Force Nuclear Enterprise Funding

With focused advocacy and an increased effort to deliberately vet nuclear requirements, acquisition, and programming processes, the Air Force will ensure the appropriate level of investment in the Air Force nuclear enterprise while providing a long-term commitment to sustain, modernize, and recapitalize its nuclear capability.

- (Organization, Leadership) Chief of Staff of the Air Force (CSAF) will designate a senior leader who will be responsible to advocate on behalf of the entire Air Force nuclear enterprise during requirements, acquisition, and programming processes. This leader will be responsible for collecting data on Air Force nuclear enterprise risk and resource options, and for formulating a comprehensive POM position which adequately captures the impact of resource decisions across the Air Force nuclear enterprise. This senior leader must also be a member of and/or represented at every level of the requirements process so that requirements match advocacy for nuclear issues presented to the AFCS. The Air Force nuclear enterprise funding leader must be responsible for ensuring all levels of the AFCS are made aware of any issues with regards to the Air Force nuclear enterprise requirements, acquisition, and programming processes. (BRR-05, -30, -32; CANS-01; DSB-08, -08c; Schlesinger Report-01, -08, -09, -10, -20, -31, -32) Action *Complete—See Chapter 7* (AFI 16-501; AF/A10 Implementing Directive)

- (Organization, Leadership) Air Force Strategic Plans and Programs (AF/A8) has established Headquarters Air Force Operations, Plans, and Requirements Nuclear [AF/A10 (AF/A3/5N)] leadership as a full member of the Air Force Group and Air Force Board (beta test) (BRR-30; Schlesinger Report-10) *Actions Complete* (AFI 16-501)

Air Force Requirements, Acquisition, and Programming Processes must Enhance Capabilities and Define Risk to the Air Force Nuclear Enterprise

The Air Force must create strategic investment plans that address mid-term requirements and acquisitions (i.e. F-35 dual capability, tanker replacement, and WSA alignment) and long-term requirements and acquisition strategies (i.e. ALCM, bomber, and ICBM replacements) to ensure future viability of our nuclear deterrent forces. The AFCS must know which Program Elements (PE) comprise the Air Force nuclear enterprise and fully understand the implications of resource decisions. There must be a thorough analysis of funding across the entire Air Force nuclear enterprise. Additionally, some program elements will not be directly attributed to the Air Force nuclear enterprise, but will impact it through the infrastructure and sustainment links.

- (Doctrine, Organization) AF/A8 is currently evaluating the portfolios of the existing 12 panels of the AFCS to identify PEs which directly or indirectly impact and comprise the Air Force nuclear enterprise. (BRR-28, -31; CANS-03) *Complete by Dec 2008* (AFI 16-501)

- (Doctrine, Organization) AF/A8 is currently evaluating the consolidation of all nuclear-related PEs into one panel, or a similarly robust management portfolio. (BRR-28, -31; CANS-03) *Complete by Dec 2008* (AFI 16-501)

- (Doctrine, Organization) AF/CV will direct evaluation of a "beta-test" Virtual Major Force Program (vMFP) dedicated to the Air Force Nuclear Enterprise in order to consolidate all nuclear-related programs into one robust management and data repository—pending evaluation of "beta-test," coordinate final recommendation and request approval to establish an Air Force Nuclear Enterprise vMFP to OSD/PA&E. (AFNTF) *Complete within 12 months* (AFI 16-501)

- (Organization, Leadership) CSAF will direct AF/A3/5 to align nuclear enterprise requirements and capability champions processes to mirror any changes to the PE and panel structure within the AFCS. (BRR-28, -31; CANS-03) *Complete within 6 months* (AFI 16-501)

- (Organization, Leadership) SecAF will direct SAF/AQ & SAF/USA to align nuclear enterprise acquisition processes to mirror the revised AFCS process. (BRR-28, -31; CANS-03) *Complete within 6 months* (AFI 16-501)

Manage Final Budget and Execution in the Air Force Nuclear Enterprise

In order to ensure we allocate and execute resources with a full understanding of the Air Force nuclear enterprise, the AFCS must consider current budget execution in addition to the POM process.

- (Doctrine, Organization) AF/A10 (AF/A3/5N) will develop a process to ensure Air Force nuclear enterprise risk is adequately considered and vetted when resources are redirected to more urgent priorities during budget execution. (AFNTF) *Complete within 6 months* (AFI 16-501)

Chapter 6 — Advocacy Across the Air Force Nuclear Enterprise

> *Deterrence is not just aircraft on alert and missiles in the silos. It is not defined by the size of the defense budget. It is the product of both capability and credibility.*
>
> *General Jerome F. O'Malley*

Problem Statement

The Air Force does not demonstrate sustained advocacy and commitment to the nuclear deterrence mission while helping to win today's fight.

Success Criteria and Desired Sub-Objectives

This chapter discusses the lack of advocacy in many forms including organization, accountability and culture, expertise, investment, and strategic communication. The action plan presented in this chapter is specific to strategic communication and presents a phased plan for the Air Force institution and leadership to correct the deficiency. Other advocacy-related action items in categories such as organization and investment are presented in their respective chapters of this roadmap.

Advocacy is necessary to reinvigorate the Air Force nuclear enterprise. Success in the Air Force nuclear enterprise will be apparent when confidence and credibility are restored, the importance of the mission is elevated, Airmen are consistently held accountable for their actions, and the Air Force re-commits itself as the nation's enduring sole provider of nuclear deterrence weapons launched from US soil.

Communicating our message is a key component of advocacy. We must inform key audiences such as Airmen at all levels, Air Force senior leaders, Congress, OSD, Joint Staff, COCOMs, national leaders, think tanks, influencers, allies and partners, and the American public about the importance of the Air Force nuclear enterprise. In addition to measuring opinion and attitude shifts, success will be measured according to how well the specific actions outlined in this roadmap are executed and how well those actions strengthen the Air Force nuclear enterprise.

To communicate the Air Force commitment to re-invigorating the Air Force nuclear enterprise, Secretary of the Air Force Directorate of Communication and Public Affairs, in coordination with the Special Assistant for Air Force Strategy, AF/A8, AF/A10 (AF/A3/5N), and MAJCOM CCs , will create a coordinated, advocacy-based engagement strategy that enables thoughtful Air Force input to national and joint policy, strategy and planning processes, and puts the Air Force on notice that real, enduring changes and improvements are needed throughout the Air Force nuclear enterprise.

Root Causes

Perspective and History: The Erosion of Advocacy

Advocacy for the Air Force nuclear mission fragmented over the past two decades as the role of nuclear weapons in deterrence slipped in national priority. Since the end of the Cold War, the strategic environment and associated national security strategy de-emphasized nuclear deterrence. Specifically, the threat of state-state nuclear war has diminished, driving major changes in Air Force priorities and organization.

- The quality and credibility of US nuclear forces are critical to an effective deterrence (Schlesinger Report)

- Senior leadership decisions have had the cumulative effect of compromising the Air Force's deterrence capabilities (Schlesinger Report)

- There has been a steady long-term trend minimizing the perceived importance of the nuclear deterrence to national security (DSB)

Air Force MAJCOM restructuring in the 1990s led to fragmentation of advocacy. The Air Force MAJCOM reorganization was quickly followed by the fundamental re-posturing of the Air Force into an expeditionary force. This was perhaps just as significant as the MAJCOM restructure due to the shift of people, resources, and priorities to conventional operations.

- No single command to advocate for the resources required to support nuclear capabilities (Schlesinger Report)

- Nuclear missions became embedded in organizations whose primary focus is not nuclear (Schlesinger Report)

- By embedding nuclear mission forces in non-nuclear enterprise, and a general devaluation of the nuclear mission and those who perform the mission (DSB)

- Current USAF nuclear organizational construct fragments nuclear weapons advocacy and policy (BRR)

Unintended Consequences: The Leadership and Investment Bathtub

Given the national importance of the nuclear enterprise, the Air Force must develop leaders who understand and value the nuclear mission. Without a senior Air Force nuclear enterprise leader at the three- or four-star level, it may be difficult to develop future leaders within the nuclear enterprise. With a senior mentor, junior Airmen will better recognize the nuclear mission's importance. With a larger cadre of personnel with nuclear expertise who value the mission, the Air Force will be able to populate key joint nominative billets with Airmen who are also advocates of the nuclear enterprise.

- It is essential that leaders restore discipline and pride among the Airmen who perform the Air Force's nuclear mission (Schlesinger Report)

- The imperative to ensure discipline in regard to adherence to regulations and technical data needs to be constantly reinforced by supervisors and commanders (BRR)

With the restructuring of nuclear forces and equipment into multiple organizations, combined with a new expeditionary focus, the Air Force was distracted from the task of advocating for investment in the Air Force nuclear enterprise. In other words, when multiple MAJCOMs became stewards for nuclear investment, it became more challenging to advocate with one voice. Without strong investment advocacy, the Air Force budget for nuclear-related equipment, facilities, and personnel eroded.

- Underinvestment in the nuclear deterrence mission is evident, undercutting the nation's deterrence posture (Schlesinger Report)

- No comprehensive process exists to ensure sustained investment advocacy (Schlesinger Report)

Action Plan

A Strategic Communication Plan: Focus on Key Audiences

The action plans for many of the root causes listed above are answered in their respective chapters; however, advocacy in the form of a strategic communication plan will be discussed in the following paragraphs.

Advocacy for the Air Force nuclear enterprise must be executed by developing a deliberate communication plan with specific audiences in mind. In general, those audiences are the internal Air Force and the external audience, to include DoD, law- and policy-makers, and the American public. Assessing the effects of the plan over time is essential. Success will depend upon leaders matching words with deeds.

- (Doctrine, Leadership) Secretary of the Air Force Directorate of Communication and Public Affairs will develop an Air Force nuclear enterprise advocacy plan using a cyclic process of researching, planning, executing, and assessing. (DSB-08; Schlesinger Report-13, -14) *Complete within 6 months*

- (Doctrine, Organization, Leadership) SAF/CM will measure effectiveness by comparing the current level of advocacy to levels measured after the plan is implemented in the near-, medium-, and long-term horizons. (DSB-08a) *Enduring*

Near and Mid-Term Horizons: Leadership and Doctrine

Internal Air Force and external audiences will pay the most attention to actions taken sooner rather than later. Both audiences have been sufficiently informed by the actions and statements of the Secretary of Defense and accompanying media coverage to put the Air Force on notice that real, enduring changes and improvements are needed throughout the Air Force nuclear enterprise. Air Force senior leaders, to include the Secretary of the Air Force, Chief of Staff, the Under Secretary of the Air Force, and general officers (GOs) who lead elements of the Air Force nuclear enterprise, must take steps now that will plant the seeds of sustained improvement. They must be vocal, visible, and credible. Near- and mid-term outreach should first center on the internal audience. Near-term advocacy is defined as that period expiring approximately 90-days after release of the Schlesinger Panel Report, or approximately 31 December 2008. Mid-term advocacy will span the following six months, or until July 2009. This initial Air Force nuclear enterprise advocacy timeframe should focus on outreach, doctrinal revision, policy change, organizational structure, training, personnel, and leadership and education (loosely, a DOTMLPF construct).

- (Leadership) Air Force senior leaders must visit ICBM, bomber, DCA fighter, nuclear command and control, storage, and sustainment bases and facilities. During these visits, they will be prepared to speak directly to those Airmen and civilians performing missions that directly underpin the nation's nuclear deterrence credibility. They will present awards, give advocacy briefings related to the importance of the Continental United States (CONUS)-based and Outside the Continental United States (OCONUS)-based deterrence mission, and attend inspection outbriefs. (BRR-10) *Complete within 6 to 18 months—enduring*

- (Leadership) Air Force leaders will participate in outreach by writing scholarly articles for publication in the many Air Force journals, such as "Air & Space Power Journal," "Strategic Studies Quarterly," and "High Frontier." Outreach will then move to the external audience, to include law- and policy-makers, think tanks, the other Services, and the American public. The same scholarly writings will again be used for publication in "Armed Force Journal," "Joint Force Quarterly," and "Air Force Magazine." Such articles spawn op-eds, written by scholars and policy-makers, in local and national newspapers. (BRR-21) *Complete within 6 to 18 months—enduring*

- (Leadership) Air Force leaders will make public addresses on the importance of the Air Force's role as sole provider of land and air based nuclear deterrence and the steps taken to improve our stewardship of the mission. Specifically, senior uniformed and DoD civilians will speak both on and off the record with Washington, DC think tanks and universities that specialize in discussing national security topics. The result of proactive external engagement is often sustained symbiotic relationships between the Air Force and those who were, and may be, in the seats of power. (Schlesinger Report-09) *Complete within 6 to 18 months—enduring*

- (Doctrine) LeMay Center for Doctrine Development & Education (LeMay Center) will revise Air Force nuclear doctrine to reflect the renewed understanding of the mission's importance. (BRR-14) *Complete within 6 months* (AFDD 2-1.5, Nuclear Operations (soon to be redesignated AFDD 2-12))

- (Training, Leadership, Personnel) AETC/AU will ensure requisite emphasis of the nuclear mission is placed in the appropriate officer and enlisted accession training, professional military education (PME), and technical training schools. (BRR-20, Schlesinger Report-11, -19) *Complete within 6 to 18 months*

Far-Term Horizon: National Leadership Advocacy

A more demanding task for the Air Force will be to influence Joint doctrine, OSD policy, and National Security Strategy.

On the far planning horizon (July 2009 and beyond), advocacy must focus on three fronts: a budget and Congressional dialogue to reflect our nuclear priority; an Air Force cultural shift that embraces the importance of the Air Force nuclear deterrence mission; and taking account of the current benchmark for excellence, such as the US Navy's nuclear program. These three changes depend upon actions taken now, but must be monitored for continued relevance and adjusted to meet the changing context of national security threats, Presidential priorities, and the views of American society.

Dialogue with Congress must be regular, deliberate, and transparent.

- (Leadership) Secretary of the Air Force Legislative Liaison (SAF/LL) will interface with Congress on a regular basis and expand nature of dialogue to include the Air Force nuclear enterprise. (BRR-07) *Complete within 6 to 18 months— enduring* (AFI 90-402)

In addition to Congressional interface, the Air Force must also participate in debate and discussion that lends to evolution of National Security Strategy. These discussions occur between Services, the Joint community and OSD, coalition services, and other nations.

- (Leadership) Air Force senior leaders will participate in forums that bolster the Air Force role in the US nuclear deterrence mission. (BRR-29) *Complete within 6 to 18 months—enduring*

SAF/CM and AF/A10 (AF/A3/5N) will measure and track the deliverables contained in this report and determine progress of this advocacy plan.

Chapter 7 — Organizational Alternatives

> *"The art of progress is to preserve order amid change and preserve change amid order."*
>
> *Alfred North Whitehead*

Problem Statement

Air Force nuclear-related authority and responsibility are fragmented, and are not aligned with nuclear deterrence mission requirements.

Chapter Organization

To provide context that led to organizational decisions made at the 18 September 2008 Nuclear Summit/1-3 October 2008 CORONA, this chapter reflects the attributes of a composite sustainment, field operational and headquarters organizational structure required to ensure reinvigorated USAF stewardship of our nuclear deterrence mission.

Success Criteria and Methodology

No amount of change in a single organizational category (at the exclusion of corresponding change in the other categories) can address all the attributes of success across the Air Force nuclear enterprise. The attributes of success are discussed in the sections following each respective organizational change section.

The Air Force Nuclear Task Force developed a construct (Figure 7-1) for evaluating the interrelated sustainment, field operations, and headquarters elements.

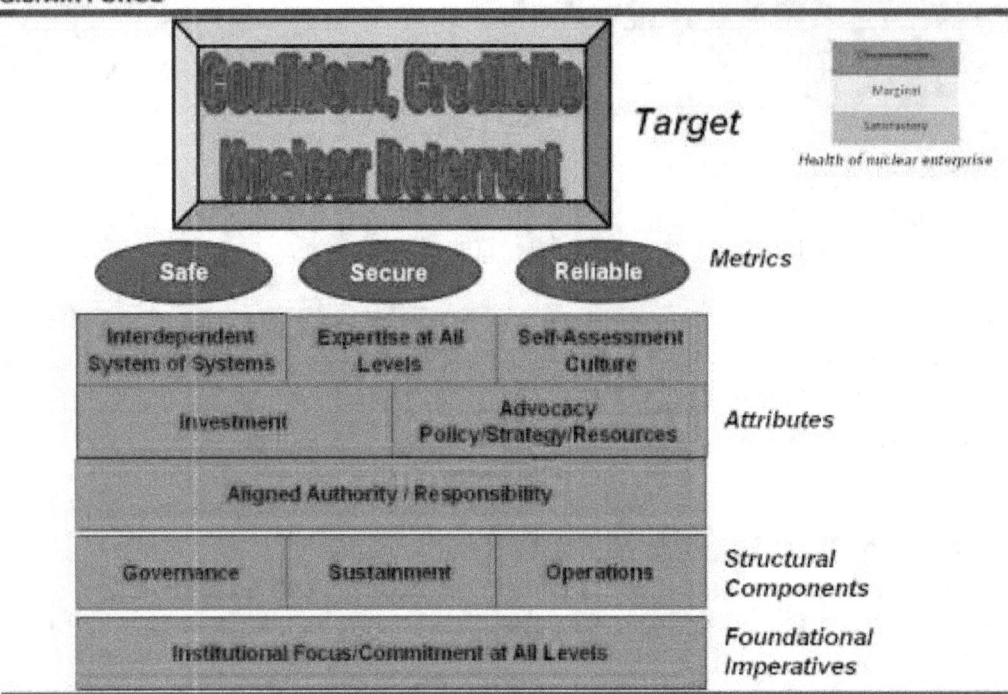

Figure 7-1: Baseline for AF Nuclear Deterrence Operations

The "Baseline for Nuclear Deterrence Operations" model has five levels:

- The first level is the foundation of the Air Force nuclear enterprise: An institutional focus and commitment to the stewardship of the nuclear mission by all Air Force personnel, from the Service Secretary and the Chief of Staff down to the newly recruited Airman in training

- The second level shows the three structural areas to implement organizational change:

  - Governance reflects changes to the higher-headquarters structure that oversees the entirety of the Air Force nuclear enterprise

  - Sustainment focuses on weapons, stockpile, and systems stewardship. Some of the systems included are warheads, ICBMs, cruise missiles, and the integration of weapons into delivery systems

  - Operations relates to the organization of fielded operational units. While this can include levels down to the squadron and below, the AFNTF narrowed the development of courses of action to MAJCOM and NAF-level structures

- The third level contains those attributes a structural component contributes to providing the desired lines of authority and responsibility vital to the nuclear enterprise. The easiest course of action is to modify one structural component to simultaneously maximize all attributes. However, that "silver bullet" does not exist. In reality, each component enhances certain attributes of the entire structure, but does not reach the same level of effectiveness that composite changes across all components can achieve

- The fourth level shows measurable qualities. The Air Force can distill metrics from these qualities to empirically evaluate how well the attributes are contributing to the overall target of the nuclear enterprise

- The fifth and final level incorporates the broader strategic targets already identified in this roadmap

Based on the combination of external reviews plus the Task Force deliberations, the "as is" Air Force nuclear deterrence picture is shown in Figure 7-2. This stands in contrast to Figure 7-1 and shows there is a critical need for reinvigorating the Air Force nuclear enterprise now.

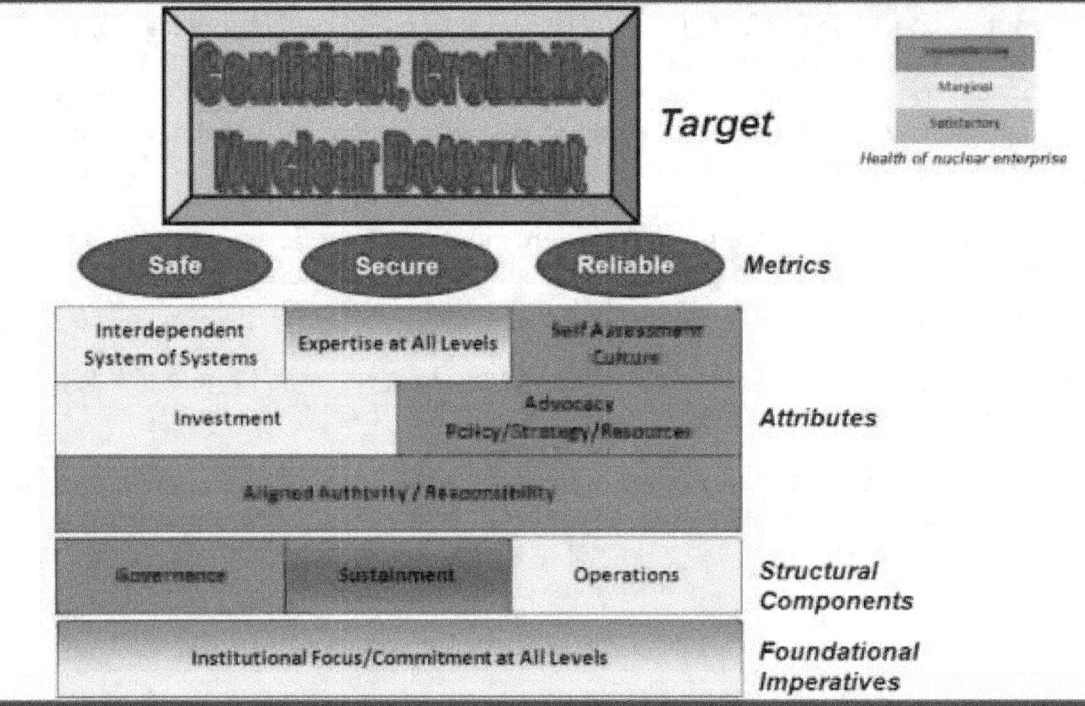

Figure 7-2: Current Assessment of AF Nuclear Deterrence

Composite Organization

When evaluating competing component courses of action, it was important to consider the overall effects of organizational change on the Air Force nuclear enterprise. The interrelated organizational change decision considered the composite organization recommendations found in the core reports such as:

- Ensure effective nuclear operations and flawless nuclear surety

- Establish clear lines of responsibility and authority

- Air Force nuclear enterprise senior leaders must have sufficient influence over acquisition, requirements, planning programming budgeting execution (PPBE), operations, logistics, personnel, etc.

- Organization should have similar attributes to the Navy's Strategic Systems Program (SSP)

- Must be properly sized and resourced given current realities

- Must retain a robust Washington, DC presence to effectively engage with mission partners

The insights gained from the internal/external reviews, additional considerations such as protecting our ability to support the current fight, enhancement of domain excellence, etc; and USAF-leadership approved organizational attributes formed the foundation for a composite organizational approach with sustainment, field operational, and headquarters elements.

Sustainment Organization

Attributes of a Successful Sustainment Enterprise

Two key attributes were identified to ensure successful management of the nuclear sustainment enterprise with the second attribute highlighting six critical functions.

- A single center responsible for sustainment of nuclear weapons and related nuclear certified systems

- A single center led by a General Officer (GO)/Senior Executive Service (SES) for nuclear weapons and systems sustainment which provides:

  - Systems engineering for nuclear weapons sustainment, certification, and weapons effects

  - Overall system management for Air Force nuclear weapons, ICBMs, cruise missiles, aircraft weapons interface, and weapons trainers

  - Programmatic and technical leadership for sustainment of all Air Force nuclear weapons, ICBMs, cruise missiles, aircraft weapons interface, and weapons trainers

  - Funding advocacy for the nuclear sustainment enterprise

  - Oversight of nuclear facility infrastructure – facility certification (i.e., ICBM Launch Facilities, Launch Control Centers and Launch Critical Infrastructure); tracks storage facility deviations for CSAF; new facility designs

  - Nuclear unique and nuclear-related support equipment management with cognizance of dual-use nuclear certified support equipment

Sustainment Organization Course of Action

After analyzing several COAs, Air Force senior leadership chose to place the AFNWC under AFMC which is consistent with the Dr. Schlesinger's Task Force Report recommendations. Under this COA, the commander for AFMC will serve as the lead agent for Air Force nuclear weapons and nuclear weapons-related materiel (as shown in Figure 7-3).

The portfolio of the AFNWC's plan for Phase I and II includes all responsibilities needed to sustain nuclear weapons and related nuclear certified systems for 1) Life Cycle Support; 2) Stockpile Stewardship; 3) Nuclear Engineering; and 4) Nuclear Facility Management. The Schlesinger Panel also recommended that the CSAF direct the consolidation of CONUS and USAFE-controlled weapons storage areas under the AFNWC and the realignment of functions associated with ICBMs and cruise missiles, including Program Executive Officer (PEO) responsibilities. Realignment of PEO authority for ICBMs and cruise missiles is currently being analyzed for implementation in Phase IV of the Air Force Nuclear Weapons Center implementation plan. The recommendation to consolidate OCONUS weapon storage areas under the AFNWC will not be addressed in this roadmap but has been tasked to the USAFE/CC for assessment and recommendation. All assessments and recommendations will be conducted with full transparency between USAFE and the host nations.

Under AFNWC Phase III, responsibility for all CONUS-based nuclear weapons maintenance, storage, accounting, moving, handling, and control will belong to AFMC. Specifically, AFNWC will provide nuclear munitions support to operational missions of Air Combat Command (ACC), Air Force Space Command (AFSPC), and ultimately Air Force Global Strike Command (AFGSC). The mission of the WSA munitions organizations under the AFNWC will be to provide operationally ready nuclear weapons when and where needed. AFNWC will provide robust nuclear weapons maintenance management capability across the spectrum of operational and sustainment requirements. The implementation of AFNWC Phase III will provide focused and enhanced oversight and standardization of nuclear weapons maintenance, storage, accountability and control, integrate the AF's CONUS nuclear sustainment capabilities in support of the combatant commander through the full range of Air Force strategic operations and align our peacetime train and equip organization to safely, securely, and reliably meet the nation's strategic deterrence posture while continuing to prepare for and, when necessary, conduct warfighting operations.

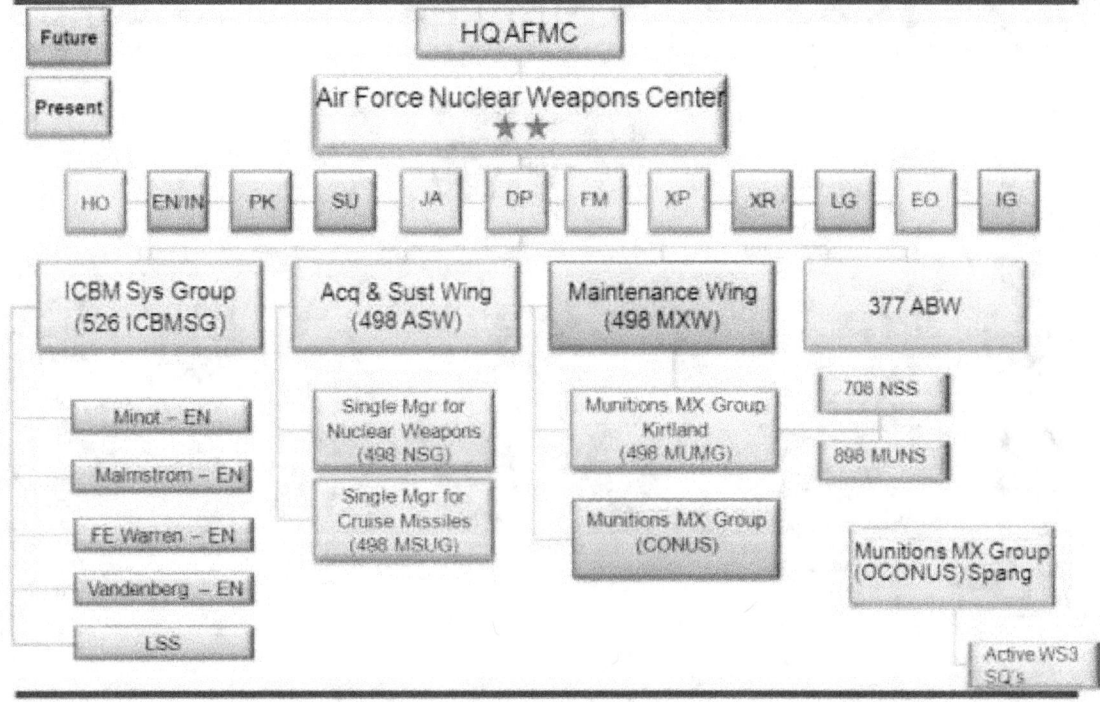

Figure 7-3: Air Force Nuclear Weapons Center (AFNWC)

Air Force Sustainment Organization Action Plan

The Air Force has directed the AFMC commander serve as the lead agent for Air Force nuclear weapons and nuclear weapons-related materiel. AFMC/AFNWC reorganization consolidated the 526th ICBM Systems Group; with draft plans to incorporate wing-level technical engineering support under the 526th ICBM Systems Group. Realignment of PEO authority for ICBMs and cruise missiles is currently being analyzed for implementation in Phase IV of the Air Force Nuclear Weapons Center implementation plan.

The Air Force has directed the consolidation of all CONUS-based WSAs under AFNWC, as discussed earlier. However, a decision to consolidate USAFE-controlled weapons storage under the AFNWC will not be made until a full analysis is conducted on the potential impacts on the USAFE mission and that of our allies. Additionally, AFMC and AFSPC will conduct an analysis to determine a way ahead regarding the requirement and feasibility of realigning the Space and Missile Center from AFSPC to AFMC.

Air Force Field Operations Organization

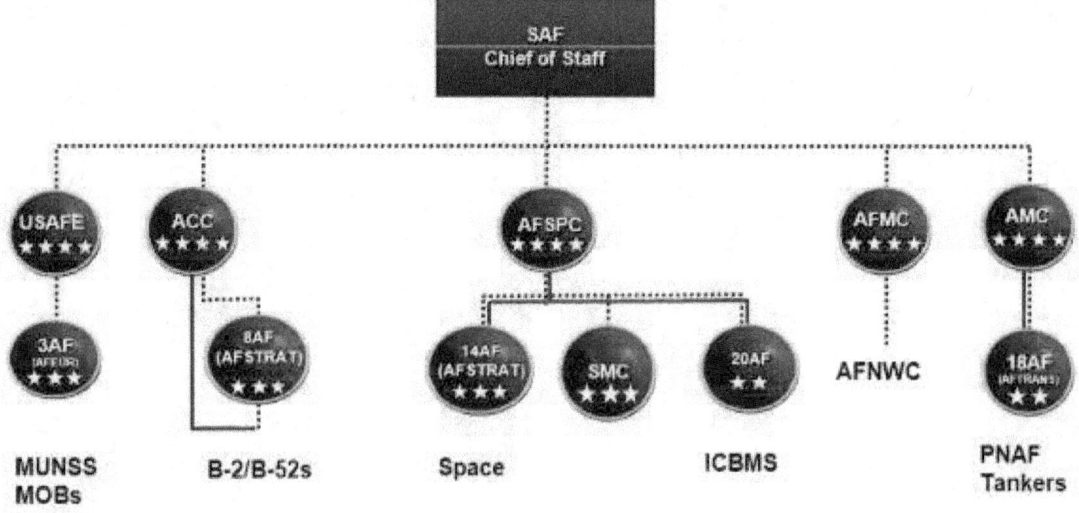

Figure 7-4: Current Nuclear-Focused Command Relationships

Attributes of Successful Field Operations Organizational Structure

In developing COAs to solve the field operations organizational issue, the following attributes were identified:

- Clear lines of authority with dedicated nuclear focus

  - Single chain: mission authority, responsibility, and accountability

  - Culture of compliance and primacy for the nuclear deterrence mission

- Advocacy/Influence

  - Resources...advocate mission requirements

  - Influence manpower, policy, and strategy decisions

  - Long-range planning, funding, and readiness

- o System-of-systems enhancements

- Seamless integration with HAF and AFNWC

  - o HAF influence…application of AF capability across full range of national security objectives

- AF-wide expertise + robust force development

- Coherent presentation of strategic deterrence capability…shape COCOM plans

- Ensure readiness: test, exercises, inspections, and requirements

- Authority/assets to drive culture of compliance

- Posture AF for rapidly changing global environment

- Enable suite of global options for crisis management

Field Operations Organization Course of Action

The Air Force considered several reorganization alternatives to reinvigorate the nuclear enterprise as part of the roadmap development. The field operations organization attributes used to develop, analyze, and compare the organizational alternatives were derived from the findings of the ADM Donald, Defense Science Board (Gen Welch), Blue Ribbon Review reports, Dr. Schlesinger's Task Force Report, as well as inputs from nuclear MAJCOM staffs. In developing the COAs, the Air Force gave careful consideration to the Schlesinger Panel Report recommendations concerning the Air Force organization construct; 1) The SecAF and CSAF should redesignate Air Force Space Command as Air Force Strategic Command; 2) The SecAF and CSAF should direct the assignment of all Air Force bombers to 8th Air Force; 3) the SecAF and CSAF should direct the removal of all non-bomber related missions from 8th Air Force; 4) the SecAF and CSAF should direct the reassignment of the reconstituted 8th Air Force from Air Combat Command to Air Force Strategic Command.

During CORONA (1-3 October 2008), based on a careful assessment of the previously mentioned attributes as well as other relevant considerations, USAF leadership approved the following operational command structure (Figure 7-5):

Nuclear/Strategic MAJCOM

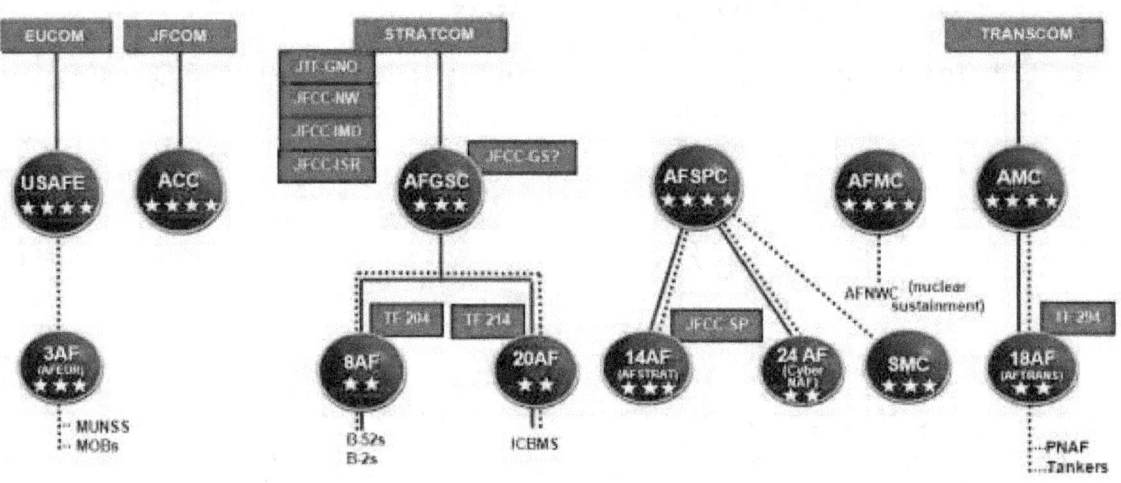

Figure 7-5: Nuclear/Strategic MAJCOM

This organizational construct clearly aligns nuclear operational units under a single command and demonstrates a visible, bold commitment to the nuclear deterrence and global strike missions while taking full advantage of the existing Air Force field organizational structure. The establishment of AFGSC will not include DCA fighters and will have no impact on USAFE operations. All nuclear organize, train, and equip functions, to include the implementation and execution of a Global Deterrence Force (GDF), will be the responsibility of the AFGSC/CC. In this role, AFGSC could provide value-added support to USAFE in the form of standards integration and nuclear mission requirements advocacy. Additionally, where required and beneficial to the AFGSC's focus on nuclear deterrence and global strike mission responsibilities, designated functions (CAF support for conventional operations, etc) will be supported through relationships with existing commands. By keeping the operational focus on the nuclear mission, AFGSC will be able to foster a robust nuclear culture, as well as establish an effective self-assessment culture. Finally, in order to ensure optimum execution of the GDF and to achieve a proper balance between the nuclear/strategic deterrence mission and today's current fight, the activation of a fourth B-52 Squadron will be critical to the success of the GDF.

AF/A10 will be the OPR for Program Action Directive (PAD) development and has formed an integrated product team to finalize roles and responsibilities as well as identify what units will be assigned to AFGSC. Development and implementation of the PAD may require the near-term establishment of a provisional AFGSC organization and designation of a provisional commander. This provisional commander will be responsible for implementing the associated PAD and prepare the command for activation.

Air Force Field Operations Organization Action Plan

The USAF will:

- o Stand up a new MAJCOM (AFGSC), dedicated to the nuclear and global strike missions. Projected IOC September 2009. AFGSC will consist of 8th AF (B-2s and B-52s) and 20th AF (ICBMs)

- o All ISR, command and control platforms and cyber assets will be removed from 8th AF

- o As part of the program action directive guidance, the Air Force will direct a review of the manning requirements for the AFGSC, ACC, 8th AF, and 20th AF headquarters as well as the assigned wings under Air Force Global Strike Command

Air Force Headquarters Organization

Current Air Force Headquarters Structure

The current Air Force headquarters organizational structure consolidates the Air Force nuclear enterprise office within the Operations and Requirements directorate (AF/A3/5) as a matrixed entity, made up of dedicated personnel from AF/A3/5N and non-dedicated personnel from across the headquarters. This construct is indicative of the fragmentation of the Air Force nuclear enterprise at the headquarters level.

Current A3/5N Organization

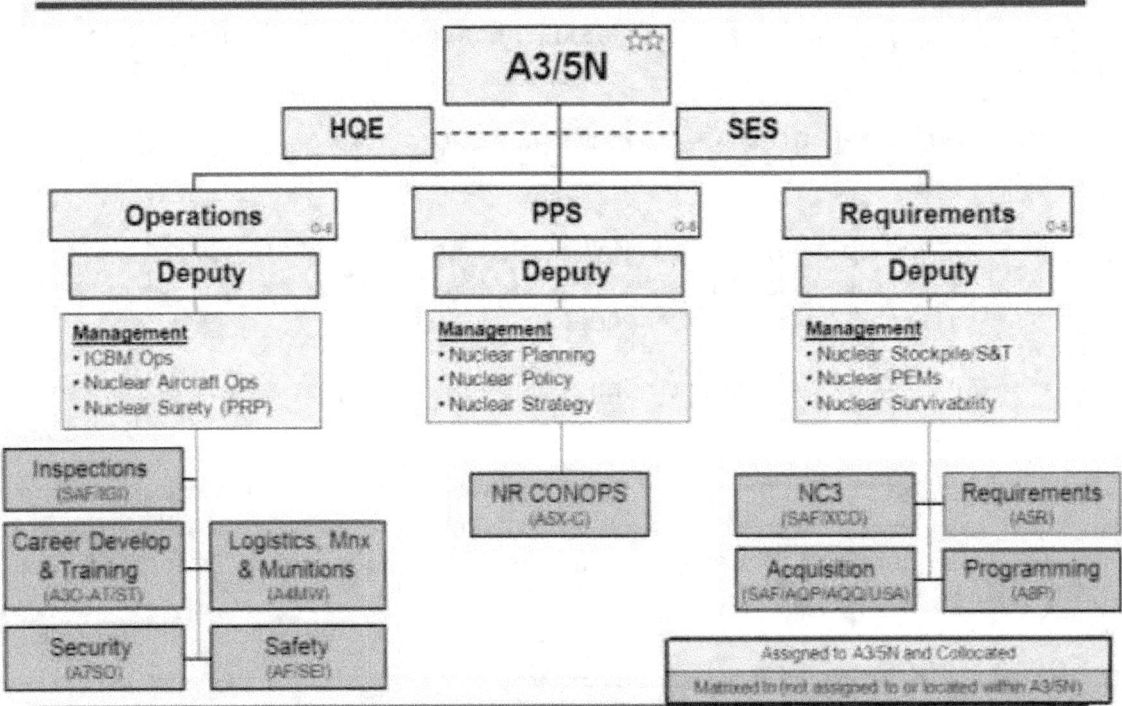

Integrity - Service - Excellence

Figure 7-6: Current Air Force Headquarters Nuclear Structure

Attributes of Successful Air Force Headquarters Nuclear Structure

Unlike Air Force domain operations, the Headquarters Air Force structure to manage the Air Force nuclear enterprise suffers from organizational weakness across the Air Staff. In developing COAs to solve the headquarters' organizational issue, the key attributes used to evaluate the various COAs were:

- Visible Air Force commitment

- Direct access to the SecAF/CSAF

- Coordination with MAJCOM(s) to develop operational requirements

- Advocate requirements within the AFCS to ensure appropriate level of investment

- Advocate with DC-based mission partners and Congress

- Posture Air Force for rapidly changing global environment

- o Nuclear Posture Review (NPR), Quadrennial Defense Review (QDR), National Military Strategy (NMS), etc., inputs

- o Threat Reduction Advisory Committee (TRAC), Nuclear Weapons Council, ongoing Forums

- o Unified Command Plan (UCP), Arms Control, etc., for inputs

- o Global options for crisis mitigation

- Sustained USAF leadership focus

  - o Culture of primacy for the nuclear deterrence mission...top to bottom

- Orchestrate on-going assessments/root cause analysis

- Objective arbitrator for nuclear issues and nuclear clearing house

- Lead Headquarters Air Force nuclear enterprise

  - o Oversee action items performance

  - o Integrate functionally-based guidance and standards

  - o Develop, align, and present speeches, testimonies, and positions for the Air Force nuclear enterprise

Air Force Headquarters Course of Action

At the Nuclear Summit held 18 September 2008, a decision was made to create a new AF/A10 headquarters directorate. The establishment of the AF/A10 sends a clear and visible signal that the Air Force is committed to resolving the fragmented lines of authority across all levels of the nuclear enterprise and provides a headquarters Assistant Chief of Staff (ACS) that reports directly to the CSAF with authority to drive nuclear enterprise policy, guidance, requirements, and advocacy across the HAF staff. The AF/A10 will have direct access to the CSAF and SecAF and be responsible for nuclear related issues and will have lead responsibilities for nuclear plans, policy, and requirements. In addition, the AF/A10 will be responsible for the synchronization and integration of all related issues across the nuclear enterprise. The ACS will have the status of the other HAF ACS/DCSs and will have the same voting authority as other ACS/DCSs in the Air Force Corporate Structure. In addition to the AF/A10 staff, the ACS will be supported by a combined SAF/HAF nuclear issues resolution/integration team that is patterned after a current successful template used to work cross Headquarters (SAF and HAF) issues while enabling institutional focus at both the Secretary of the Air Force and CSAF levels.

The Air Force is strengthening nuclear oversight and policy functions by establishing a separate directorate (AF/A10) focused solely on the nuclear enterprise (Figure 7-7). Analysis of the billets required to execute the AF/A10 mission is ongoing and will be fully resourced once that number is validated. AF/A10 is required to stand up by 1 November 2008.

The Secretary of the Air Force will charge the Under Secretary of the Air Force with broad ongoing policy and oversight responsibilities for the nuclear enterprise. To facilitate this, the Under Secretary will be provided with a senior member of the Senior Executive Service, and appropriate supporting staff.

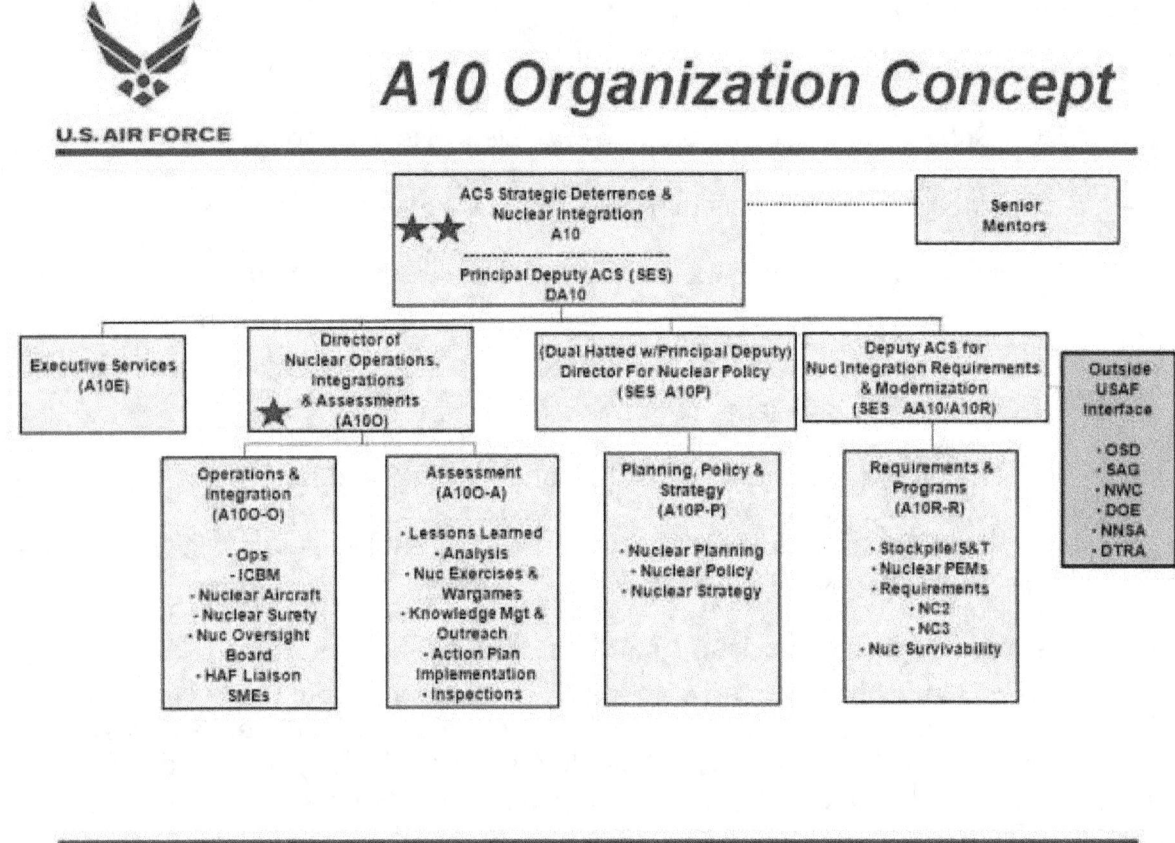

Figure 7-7: New HAF Directorate

Air Force Headquarters Organization Action Plan

- (Organization, Personnel) AF/A3/5 in partnership with AF/A1 developed, assessed, and recommended an Air Force Headquarters construct for SecAF & CSAF approval. (AFNTF) *Action 1 November 2008*

- (Organization) CSAF designated a headquarters organizational structure that includes attributes previously listed. (ADM Donald Report) *Action Complete*

- SAF/AA, in coordination with AF/A10 (AF/A3/5N), will finalize details including manning, location, CONOPs, etc.

In addition to standing up the A10 and forming the SAF/HAF Nuclear Oversight Board, Air Force senior leadership will determine final details of the Under Secretary's broad policy and oversight responsibilities on behalf of the Secretary of the Air Force (including supporting staff structure).

The combination of all the headquarters initiatives will provide a robust SAF/HAF governance structure to ensure appropriate civilian oversight and sustained reporting of the health of the nuclear enterprise to the CSAF and SecAF while precluding fragmentation of nuclear-related accountability at Headquarters USAF.

Summary

In summary, based on a leadership-approved set of attributes plus insights gained from external/internal reviews and additional considerations such as protecting USAF capability to support the current fight, the USAF will pursue a composite sustainment, field operational and headquarters' structure designed to enable the reinvigoration of the USAF Nuclear Enterprise (Figure 7-8).

- Establish a way ahead and provide resources for the AFNWC expansion of nuclear sustainment responsibilities including warhead maintenance and tracking

- Establish an AFGSC with clear lines of authority enabling a dedicated focus on the nuclear and global strike missions

- Create a Headquarters Air Force organization, AF/A10 focused on operations, policy, plans, requirements, strategy, guidance, integration, and synchronization of the nuclear enterprise

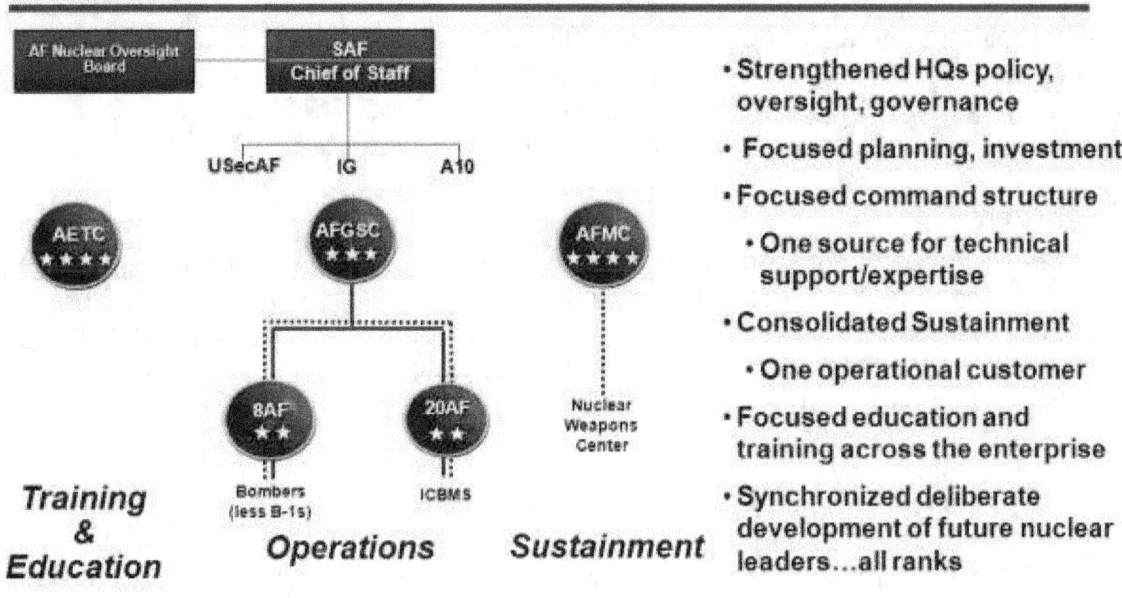

Organizational Summary

U.S. AIR FORCE

- Strengthened HQs policy, oversight, governance
- Focused planning, investment
- Focused command structure
  - One source for technical support/expertise
- Consolidated Sustainment
  - One operational customer
- Focused education and training across the enterprise
- Synchronized deliberate development of future nuclear leaders...all ranks

Integrity - Service - Excellence

Figure 7-8: Composite USAF Organizational Approach

Chapter 8 — Assessment

Introduction

On 12 August 2008, then-Acting Secretary of the Air Force Donley drew an important distinction between the Air Force conventional mission and its nuclear mission. He stated, "There has been, for a variety of reasons, a culture of needing to manage risk and to take risk across a lot of different mission areas in the Air Force mission set that we can't always meet at a hundred percent." Secretary Donley continued, "But on the nuclear side, it's really such an important mission that we shouldn't be managing risk. We should be eliminating risk. And this is what we need to get back to." The goal of risk elimination requires identifying all potential risks and analyzing the impact of our actions on the nuclear mission. We must continually strive to reduce existing and new risks to the extent possible. This is a never-ending task since all risk can not be completely eliminated.

Nuclear operations demand robust, standardized, stable, and even redundant processes and procedures in many critical areas in order to reduce risk to the lowest possible level. Risk reduction costs—both financially and in terms of mission flexibility and versatility. This "purposeful inefficiency" is required to provide the level of safety and surety demanded by the American people. This chapter presents the Air Force's assessment approach, which is similar to a balanced scorecard, to ensure we achieve and maintain the needed standards.

Success Criteria

Success in the Air Force nuclear enterprise depends on attaining and maintaining performance objectives at all levels. Initially, the assessment focus is on evaluating implementation of this roadmap and adjusting action plans where necessary. The assessment process identifies and measures the progress made toward reinvigorating the Air Force nuclear enterprise and meeting strategic objectives described in the preceding chapters. Future assessments need to go beyond the strategic findings and evaluate the entire Air Force nuclear mission.

Assessment Method

The Air Force requires an assessment method capable of measuring the progress made to improve the nuclear enterprise through the nuclear roadmap action plans. The assessment process uses measures of performance (MOPs) that address the roadmap's objectives/sub-objectives and measures of effectiveness (MOEs) that evaluate the continued accomplishment of a safe, secure, effective, and efficient nuclear mission. The MOPs indicate how well the Air Force is implementing the nuclear roadmap's objectives, and the MOEs assess how well the Air Force is accomplishing the overall objective of a safe, secure, effective, and efficient nuclear mission. In simple terms, the MOPs depict if the Air Force is doing things right, and the MOEs indicate if the Air Force is doing the right things. Various subject matter experts (SMEs) and leaders throughout the nuclear enterprise need to agree on the particular measures.

The evaluation of the measures will deliver a precise and objective assessment of the nuclear roadmap's health and highlight areas where additional progress is still required.

Before identifying the offices to implement the assessments, SMEs will evaluate and validate the MOPs (which measure objectives) and MOEs (which measure mission effects). SMEs will also propose the scoring formula for each measure. Air Force Senior Leadership will have approval authority for the "weights" (importance) of each measure so that scores can be combined. The weighted MOPs will produce a score for each sub-objective and an overall performance score. Similarly, the weighted MOEs will be combined for a score by major effect (safe, secure, efficient, and effective) and an overall effectiveness score. The performance scores indicate the progress on roadmap objectives while the effectiveness scores depict the achievement of tangible results from the nuclear activities. (See Appendix 2 - Methodology for greater detail.)

Following validation and leadership approval of the measures, the appropriate offices will collect the required data and construct an initial or baseline assessment. Many measures identified have not been collected and evaluated before. This first assessment will serve as the baseline comparison for future assessments to evaluate the progress made or regression on any particular objective. Leadership will direct periodic assessments to maintain visibility on current performance and to track trends. Figure 8-1 shows one possible approach to depicting the impact of the roadmap over time.

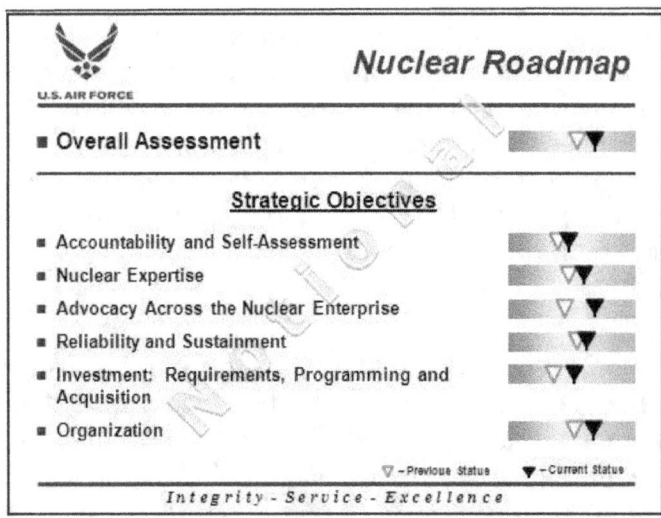

Figure 8-1: Notional Operational Assessment Stoplight Chart

Assessment scores evaluate whether the actions being performed in the nuclear enterprise are achieving the desired sub-objectives and effects. If the nuclear enterprise is implementing the action plans intended to eliminate root causes and the assessment indicates the enterprise is failing to achieve its objectives or desired effects, then leaders need to re-assess the applicable action plans or appropriateness of implemented measures. Lack of improvement in the performance measures may indicate that the action plans are either not being implemented appropriately or they are not correcting the root cause of the report findings. Similarly, poor results in the effects measures would cause an investigation into the results of action plans or an examination for new challenges in the nuclear enterprise. Leaders must review the measures and their weights periodically to ensure that the appropriate aspects of the enterprise are being addressed. Once new procedures are institutionalized, some measures may become unnecessary or experience may indicate the need for revision or additional measures. Since the roadmap has focused on correcting known problems, another reason for adding additional measures would be to broaden the scope of the assessment to encompass the entire nuclear mission. Hence, future assessments need to expand beyond the nuclear roadmap to ensure the Air Force does not regress on tasks that have been successfully accomplished over the years.

Figure 8-2 depicts the process to perform overall assessment.

Current requirements will drive the following schedule: Data collection will be completed at the wing and MAJCOM level and submitted to Headquarters Air Force quarterly for assessment and feedback. This will allow Air Force leadership to analyze progress and provide updates to external oversight committees (i.e. NSPD-28 Oversight Committee (NOC), Nuclear Oversight Board (NOB), etc.)

In the long term, data collection will be completed at the wing and MAJCOM level. The MAJCOMs will complete the collections every quarter and submit their data to Headquarters Air Force for assessment and feedback. Additionally, the Air Force will deliver status reports to external oversight committees and agencies.

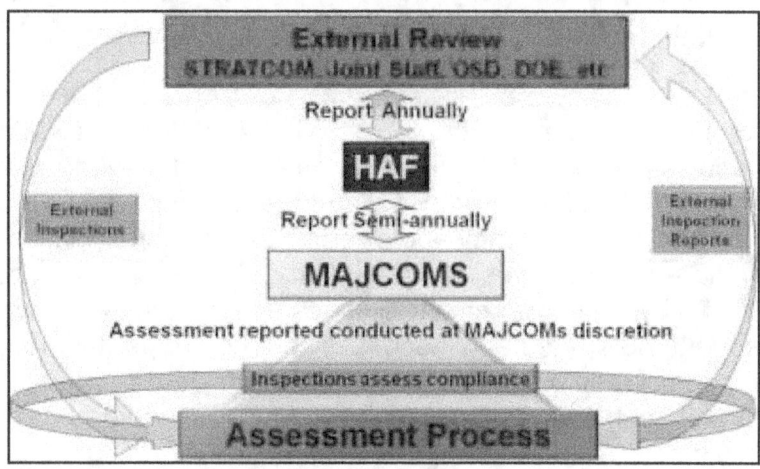

Figure 8-2: Air Force Nuclear Enterprise Assessment Process

Capturing Lessons Learned

The Air Force will capture lessons derived from implementation of the nuclear roadmap and from activities throughout the nuclear enterprise. The Air Force Lessons Learned process will assist the Air Force nuclear enterprise in applying a full range of lessons learned activities. This process assists in identifying and implementing best practices for senior decision makers, commanders, staff members, and Airmen working in the Air Force nuclear enterprise. Air Force Studies and Analyses, Assessments, and Lessons Learned (AF/A9) will assist in coordinating with the Headquarters Air Force, MAJCOMs, NAFs, centers, and agencies lessons learned offices as appropriate. The AF/A9L MAJCOM community will share lessons within the Air Force and with other joint and governmental lessons learned offices. The information gathered will provide inputs that could influence decisions across the spectrum of DOTMLPF-related policy and program areas.

The Air Force Lessons Learned process will be closely associated with identifying improvement opportunities, aggressively tracking the development of effective solutions, and disseminating lessons to the war-fighting community. AF/A9L MAJCOM community will focus on the nuclear roadmap implementation timeline and other Air Force Lessons Learned offices will assist and support when appropriate.

AF/A9L MAJCOM community will measure the effectiveness of the identified action plans based off of the suggested assessment process. Other Air Force Lesson Learned offices will assist AF/A9L with the collection effort for an independent assessment of the action plan's effectiveness. This will ensure a qualitative assessment of the relative effectiveness of various actions to feed the overall assessment process.

The most critical functions performed by the Air Force Lessons Learned community in assessing the Air Force nuclear enterprise will be the following:

- Collection: Identify and report "observations" during implementation of the nuclear roadmap and ongoing nuclear activities. Ensure lessons are documented. Disseminate "best practices" to the entire Air Force nuclear enterprise in a timely and efficient manner.

- Validation: Aggregate common observations and/or review a significant observation as a "lesson identified" or an "issue identified" and validate them at the appropriate level, usually by a Headquarters Air Force functional office. The purpose is to verify accuracy and appropriateness of an observation. Observations do not necessarily imply inadequate, incorrect, or outdated DOTMLPF. Validation also distinguishes between information and sound knowledge to be shared and lessons. The office of primary responsibility (OPR) validates the lesson or issue identified. For validated lessons, the OPR develops an approach to institutionalize that lesson. For validated issues identified, the OPR implements a resolution plan.

- Dissemination: One item highlighted by the AFNTF during its Air Force Smart Operations for the 21st Century (AFSO21) process in identifying root causes was the need to share lessons and best practices. The established and mandated method for capturing the issues which are 'Identified' and 'Lessons Identified' is through the use of the Joint Lessons Learned Information System (JLLIS). The appropriate lessons learned office disseminates formal reports to spread knowledge and experiences across the greater Air Force community.

- Tracking: To determine if a lesson was implemented, OPRs will review results and the appropriate Air Force Lessons Learned office will accomplish long-term tracking. Organizations evaluate DOTMLPF changes to determine effectiveness of these changes.

Appendix 1 — SecAF & VCSAF Guidance Letters

SecAF MEMO, Rebuilding the Nuclear Enterprise, 26 Jun 2008

SECRETARY OF THE AIR FORCE
WASHINGTON

June 26, 2008

MEMORANDUM FOR   AIR FORCE CHIEF OF STAFF
ALL MAJCOM COMMANDERS

SUBJECT: Rebuilding the Air Force Nuclear Enterprise

We are in a critical period of transition. As the acting Secretary, I need your personal support to continue mission accomplishment across the Air Force while we focus immediately on strengthening performance in our nuclear mission and determine the longer term actions necessary to rebuild the nuclear enterprise. Since September 11, 2001, our Air Force has responded with 524,000 deployments and more than 1,000,000 sorties in support of the joint fight–a contribution without which, as Secretary Gates has said, America's war effort would simply grind to a halt. I urge you to continue to lean forward in every respect in support of current joint operations.

A credible nuclear deterrent is essential to our security and that of our allies and friends. The Air Force has an essential role in this national mission. We were created as a separate Service over 60 years ago with nuclear responsibilities foremost in our mission set. There is no mission more sensitive than safeguarding our vital nuclear capabilities and maintaining nuclear deterrence. We have a sacred trust with the American people to safely operate, maintain and secure nuclear weapons. We must constantly strive for perfection in this mission area. Rigid adherence to standards, personal accountability at all levels, and leadership are the foundations upon which our success depends.

Over the past 10 months, we have received clear indicators of a decline in our nuclear mission focus and performance across our Air Force. Multiple investigations and reviews have provided both observations on our key challenges and recommendations for how to overcome identified weaknesses. Progress is being made. In recent weeks the Air Force has:

- Performed at the direction of the Secretary of Defense a comprehensive inventory of all nuclear weapons and critical and code components;
- Begun to extend positive inventory control systems and procedures to a newly defined class of nuclear weapon-related materiel;
- Consolidated all nuclear sustainment and oversight under AFMC, specifically under the Nuclear Weapons Center; and
- To improve leadership focus on nuclear matters, assigned General Officers to key positions on the air staff with singular focus on nuclear enterprise policy; to the National Nuclear Security Administration, Department of Energy; and to command and grow the Nuclear Weapons Center.

In addition, dozens of individual initiatives are now underway to improve nuclear-related policies and procedures, logistics and sustainment, and other important matters. These initiatives are necessary and should continue, but they are not sufficient.

The most important conclusions of Admiral Donald's report to the Secretary of Defense relate to systemic and institutional issues now confronting the Air Force: the well-documented decline in focus on the nuclear mission, declining nuclear expertise, and erosion of performance standards and compliance, complicated by an ineffective self-assessment culture which undermines critical self-examination and aggressive problem resolution. In particular, Admiral Donald noted split organizational authorities and responsibilities, and a lack of clarity for nuclear matters among multiple commands, as a root cause of these problems.

To build on current initiatives, integrate our collective efforts at the strategic level, and to address the cultural, systemic and institutional challenges identified in the Donald Report, I have directed the Vice Chief of Staff to establish a Nuclear Task Force to perform the following functions:

- Coordinate and synchronize the ongoing implementation of specific corrective actions underway in response to the Minot and Taiwan incidents;
- Develop in coordination with USSTRATCOM, other DoD components and interagency partners, and in all dimensions of Doctrine, Organization, Training, Materiel, Leadership, and Education, Personnel, Facilities (DOTMLPF) and the inspection process, a strategic roadmap to rebuild and restore capabilities and confidence in our stewardship of the Air Force nuclear enterprise;
- Undertake an organizational review to assess and recommend options for alternative assignments of responsibility and/or command arrangements; and
- Serve as the Air Force focal point for coordination with and/or support to other nuclear-related panels, commissions, or review groups outside the Air Force.

The Task Force will provide to me an initial progress report in 30 days and a draft roadmap, including recommendations for organizational adjustments, for the nuclear enterprise in 60 days. At that time, together with the Chief of Staff, I will assess progress and the Task Force will incorporate results from the Schlesinger Panel, recently established by the Secretary of Defense to recommend follow-on actions from Admiral Donald's report. The Task Force should then be prepared to complete deliberation within 30 days and the roadmap would be reviewed and approved at a 4-star Nuclear Summit to be scheduled in September. Supplemental guidance will be forthcoming from the Vice Chief. We will keep OSD and the Congress informed of our progress and advise them of any additional FY09/10 resource requirements that may arise.

In addition to establishing this Task Force, we must also move quickly to address the issues of accountability. Separate information will be forthcoming to affected commanders.

Our clear goal in the months ahead is to put the Air Force on the right path to correcting long-standing systemic and institutional problems in its stewardship of nuclear matters. My expectation at the end of the initial 90-day assessment period is that the USAF will be fully recommitted to the nuclear deterrent mission and its supporting elements at all levels and implementing a strategic plan to attack the root causes of past problems.

There is no question that recent events have shaken confidence in our ability to perform the nuclear mission at a level commensurate with its national importance and have damaged our credibility. We must reestablish our internal discipline, apply necessary resources, rebuild confidence, and restore our credibility. While we have important work to do at the institutional and command levels, the most direct route to improved performance is enhanced individual accountability at all levels and the raw power of thousands of Airmen, uniformed and civilian, implementing the high standards that have long been the source of the Air Force's inner strength. I know you and our Airmen understand how vital our success in this mission area is to our national security. I am confident in our ability to bounce back and am honored to join you in this important work.

Integrity first; service before self; excellence in all we do.

MICHAEL B. DONLEY
Acting Secretary of the Air Force

Cc:

SecNav
CJCS
CDR USSTRATCOM
USD(P)
USD(AT&L)
ATSD(NCB)
ASD(LA)
Dir. NNSA, DOE

VCSAF Memo, Air Force Nuclear Task Force, no date

DEPARTMENT OF THE AIR FORCE
OFFICE OF THE CHIEF OF STAFF
UNITED STATES AIR FORCE
WASHINGTON DC 20330

MEMORANDUM FOR SEE DISTRIBUTION

FROM: HQ USAF/CV
1670 Air Force Pentagon
Washington DC 20330-1670

SUBJECT: Air Force Nuclear Task Force

The Acting Secretary of the Air Force, Mr. Michael Donley, has directed me to form a task force to produce a roadmap to fortify the Air Force nuclear enterprise.

In addition to your personal views, this roadmap will be informed by the several internal and external reviews of AF nuclear programs that have been completed or are currently underway. The final Roadmap for Rebuilding the Nuclear Enterprise will be published in 90 days, with an Interim Progress Review in 30 days and draft roadmap in 60 days. The final product will contain a composite list of traceable, accountable actions that will attack our root, systemic causes and produce procedural, structural and ultimately cultural effects.

I am tasking Major General (s) Don Alston, Director of Nuclear Operations, Plans and Requirements (AF/A3/5N) to lead the Air Force Nuclear Task Force (AFNTF).

You can expect further Task Force-related guidance, to include Terms of Reference, from Gen Alston not later than 2 July 2008.

DUNCAN J. MCNABB
General, USAF
Vice Chief of Staff

Appendix 2 — Methodology

Introduction

This appendix explains the methods used in two phases: building the nuclear roadmap and assessing the roadmap implementation. The AFNTF applied a disciplined approach to determine the root causes of problems and to propose solutions. The assessment process lays out a rigorous approach to evaluate progress in correcting identified problems and improving the Air Force's ability to achieve its nuclear mission. This appendix contains three sections: 1) Use of the AFSO21 process improvement approach to construct the roadmap; 2) the resulting six comprehensive findings; and 3) the action plan assessment method.

Air Force Smart Operations for the 21st Century Process (AFSO21)

AFSO21 serves as the Air Force's Continuous Process Improvement (CPI) approach which leverages: Lean, Six Sigma, Theory of Constraints and Business Process Reengineering Improvement Methods.[4] The AFSO21 Eight-Step problem solving process is also mapped to the common military framework of the Observe, Orient, Decide, and Act (OODA) Loop Figure A2-1.

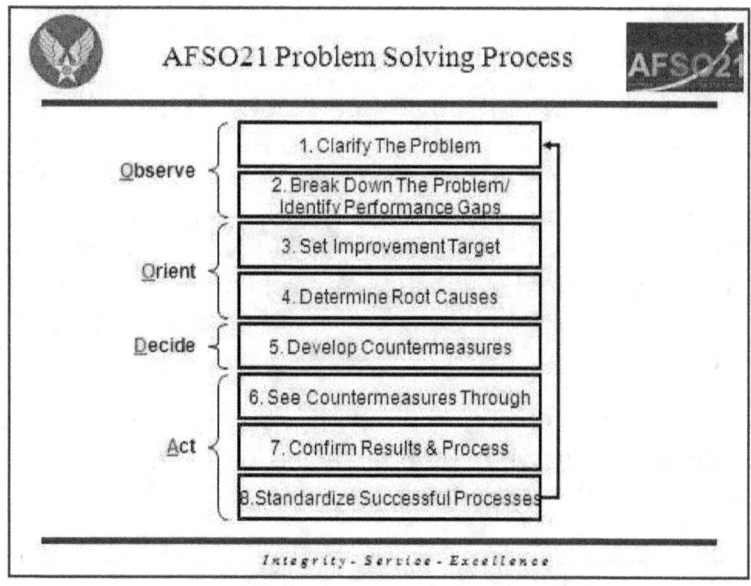

Figure A2-1: OODA Loop and the '8-Step' Process

Numerous study groups had already accomplished the Observe Phase and documented their results in reports with respective findings. Therefore, the AFNTF entered the OODA loop with these findings and focused on the Orient and Decide Phases. This section describes the activities used to determine the root causes in the Orient Phase and the development of countermeasures in the Decide Phase. Countermeasures are generally called action plans within the roadmap. The

---

[4] AFSO21 Playbook (October 2007)

assessment method described in the last section of this appendix focuses on preparing for the Act Phase.

The AFNTF consolidated and evaluated findings and recommendations from various reports, specifically the Commander Directed Investigation, Blue Ribbon Review, Defense Science Board, Air Force Inventory and Assessment, ADM Donald Report, Comprehensive Assessment of Nuclear Sustainment, and the Schlesinger Panel. The resulting 136 consolidated findings were categorized into one of seven bins:

1. Organization

2. Leadership/Culture

3. Guidance & Policy and Assessment & Oversight

4. Nuclear Mission

5. Requirements/Programs/Acquisition

6. Sustainment/Modernization

7. Personnel/Education/Training

The AFNTF assembled a working group of over forty Subject Matter Experts (SMEs) to conduct root cause analysis and develop countermeasures (action plans) on each of the seven bins of findings. The SMEs represented a cross-section of the Air Force nuclear enterprise. AFSO21 experts from the Secretary of the Air Force's Smart Operations (SAF/SO) office led this 7-day event. Furthermore, the AFNTF has continued to refine this work and accomplished additional root cause analysis on subsequent reports, specifically the Report of the Secretary of Defense Task Force on DoD Nuclear Weapons Management.

For each of the bins, the AFSO21 working group determined the root causes of the consolidated report findings. As shown in Figure A2-2, they searched for primary sources in the causal chain that led to the findings.

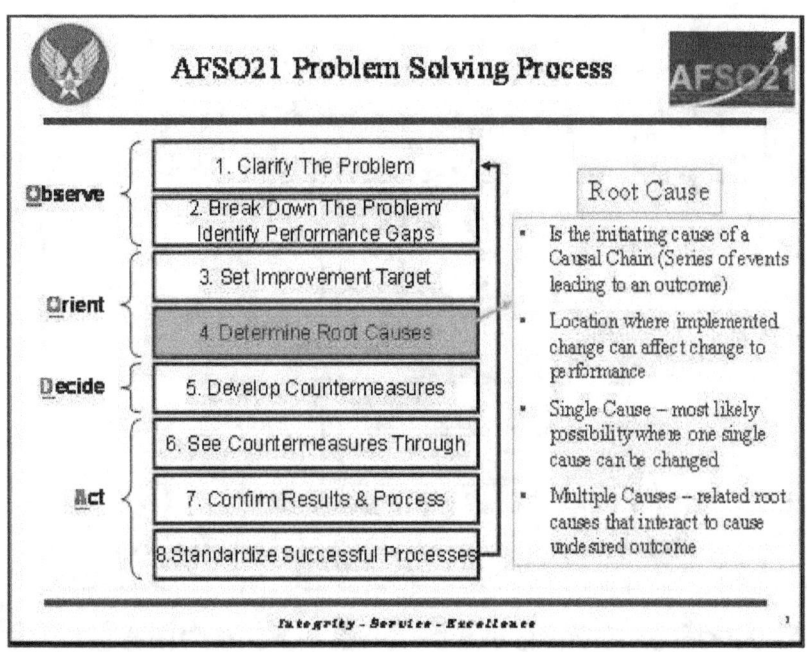

Figure A2-2: Root Cause Analysis as part of OODA Loop

The AFSO21 team primarily employed four techniques to determine root causes. First, SMEs, relying on their experiences in the Air Force nuclear enterprise, brainstormed to determine contributing causes. For postulated causes, they applied the 5 Whys approach, which repeatedly asks "why did that occur" until root causes are identified. They grouped the potential causes on Ishikawa diagrams or fishbone diagrams, which categorize the contributing causes of the findings. They also used affinity diagrams to consolidate and group similar root causes. The AFSO21 working group brainstormed countermeasures or action plans to eliminate or alleviate the impact of these root causes. Affinity diagrams were used to group the proposed action plans. The group recommended action plans deemed most likely to resolve the root causes. Figure A2-3 portrays the steps and techniques in this AFSO21 event.

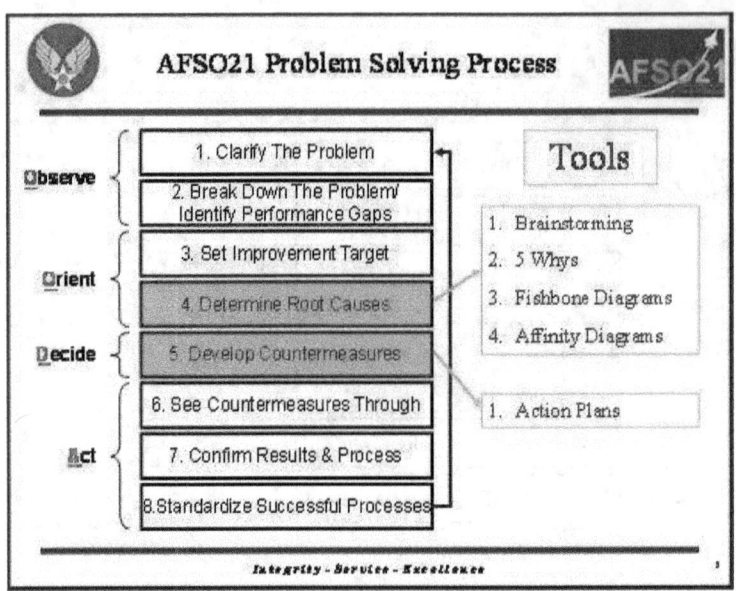

Figure A2-3: Root Cause Analysis and Developing Action Plans using AFSO21 Tools

One of the products of this review was the identification of six strategic comprehensive findings. The AFNTF writing team used the six comprehensive findings to organize the roadmap and the root-cause analysis as the foundation for each chapter.

Comprehensive Findings

The AFNTF consolidated and evaluated findings and recommendations from the previously listed reports. From the report findings, the AFNTF employed six comprehensive findings as a management construct to organize and guide roadmap development. The comprehensive findings were:

- Air Force nuclear-related authority and responsibility are fragmented/not aligned with nuclear deterrence mission demands/requirements/expectations

- The Air Force does not have a comprehensive Air Force nuclear enterprise methodology/discipline to insure day-to-day excellence as measured in the field

- Air Force nuclear-related expertise has eroded to the point that multiple positions throughout the enterprise reflect a requirement/assignment mismatch

- Air Force processes for uncovering, analyzing, addressing, and reviewing systemic weaknesses (self-assessment/culture) are ineffective

- The Air Force has underinvested in the nuclear deterrence mission and has no clear, long-term commitment to recapitalize, refresh, or replace current nuclear capability

- The Air Force does not have a comprehensive process for ensuring sustained advocacy, focus, and commitment to the nuclear deterrence mission while helping to win today's fight

A10

Each comprehensive finding was rewritten into a positive statement and became a strategic objective of the roadmap. These six strategic objectives, along with fourteen sub-objectives, will correct the six comprehensive findings. The six strategic objectives are:

- The Air Force will implement effective processes for uncovering, analyzing, addressing, and reviewing systemic weaknesses

- The Air Force will sufficiently invest in the nuclear deterrence mission arena

- The Air Force will implement comprehensive process for ensuring sustained advocacy, focus, and commitment

- The Air Force will develop adequate nuclear-related expertise and ensure positions throughout the enterprise reflect a proper match-up of requirements and assignments

- The Air Force will implement an end-to-end inter-related, systems, life-cycle nuclear enterprise methodology/discipline

- The Air Force will ensure that nuclear-related authority and responsibility is un-fragmented and aligned with nuclear deterrence mission demands, requirements, and expectations

The fourteen sub-objectives (associated report findings):

- Self-assessments and root-cause analysis conducted in conjunction with nuclear inspections

- Nuclear Inspections are conducted in a standardized and consistent manner across the Air Force nuclear enterprise

- Units utilize inspections and lessons learned to improve and enhance policy and processes

- The Air Force has sufficiently invested in manpower

- The Air Force has sufficiently invested in infrastructure

- The Air Force has sufficiently invested in nuclear systems, and nuclear-related equipment

- The Air Force is focused on, and committed to, the nuclear deterrence mission

- The Air Force advocated for the nuclear deterrence mission

- Air Force nuclear enterprise personnel possess adequate levels of training, expertise, and qualifications

- Air Force nuclear enterprise leadership possesses adequate levels of training, expertise, and qualifications

- Air Force nuclear-related positions throughout the enterprise reflect a proper match-up of requirements and assignments

- The Air Force has a robust supply chain management (SCM) system with 100% visibility

- Air Force leadership communicates clear and detailed nuclear enterprise policy and guidance

- Air Force nuclear-related authority and responsibility is aligned with nuclear deterrence mission demands, requirements, and expectations

Action Plan Assessment Method

Headquarters Air Force Studies & Analyses, Assessments, and Lessons Learned (AF/A9) developed an assessment methodology that correlates with Step 7, Confirm Results and Process, of the AFSO21 process, as shown in Figure A2-4.

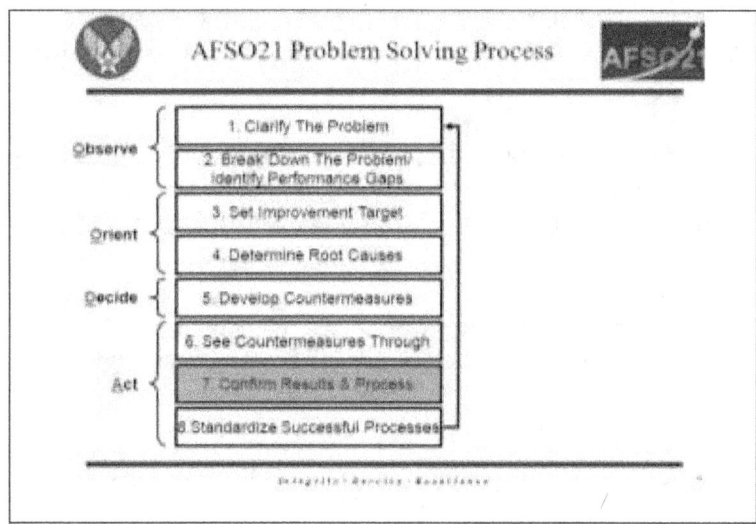

Figure A2-4: Root Cause Analysis and Developing Action Plans using AFSO21 Tools

The AF/A9 assessment approach is a variant of the value-focused thinking or the balanced scorecard techniques. The goal of this approach is to assess progress in improving the Air Force nuclear mission. The approach employs two scoring hierarchies. The first value hierarchy is based on Measures of Performance (MOPs), which assesses how well the Air Force is accomplishing tasks. The initial hierarchy was developed based on the findings (basis of the sub-objectives) from the various reports and builds to the six strategic objectives that correspond to the six comprehensive findings. If we implement the appropriate action plans, the scores in this hierarchy will improve over time. This MOP hierarchy will need to be expanded to assess the other areas of the nuclear mission that have not had problems. The second hierarchy is based on Measures of Effectiveness (MOEs), which assess how well the Air Force is accomplishing its mission. This MOE hierarchy builds to the four objectives of safe, secure, effective, and efficient. Air Force and other organizations will be able to determine the current status and trends of the nuclear mission by referring to the scores from these two hierarchies.

Figure A2-5 shows the MOP and the MOE hierarchies. The feedback arrow indicates that low scores in the Roadmap MOPs would indicate a need to investigate the implementation of the action plans or appropriateness of the measures. Low scores from the MOE hierarchy would call into question the appropriateness of the action plans. The "Ongoing" MOP hierarchy expands the approach beyond deficiencies and problems identified in the previous reports to encompass the entire nuclear mission. The following discussion will present the MOE selection and construction, evaluation, and trends.

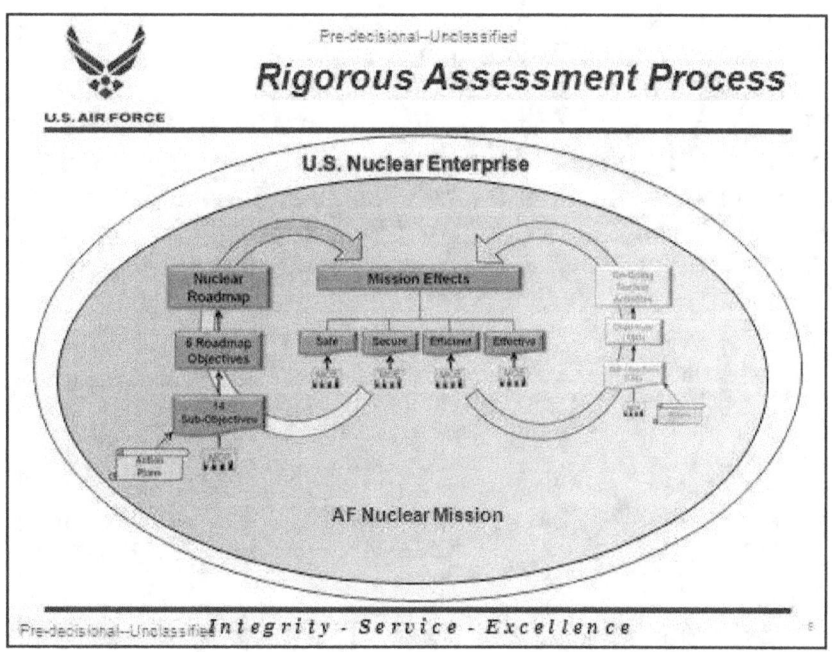

Figure A2-5: Holistic View of Assessment Process

While the AFNTF has an initial proposed set of MOPs and MOEs, the Air Force needs to agree on the selected measures to track. For each selected MOP and MOE, a scoring criterion will be established. The raw measure will be normalized to a score between zero and one. The simplest approach is a linear scoring formula

$$\text{Measure Score} = \frac{(\text{Raw Score} - \text{Worst Possible Score})}{(\text{Best Possible Score} - \text{Worst Possible Score})}$$

More complex scoring formulas will allow values higher than the desired value or lower than the least tolerable value. Scores will be scaled so that they follow a typical grading scheme.

A – Outstanding quality for scores greater than 90 percent

B – Excellent quality for scores in the range of 80 to 90 percent

C – Meets standards quality for scores in the range of 70 to 80 percent

D – Marginal quality for scores in the range of 50 to 70 percent

F – Fails standards quality for scores below 50 percent

With a consistent scoring standard, the scores for any measure immediately indicate the corresponding level of performance. The individual scores are combined to produce scores corresponding to each level of the hierarchies. This combination evaluation requires importance or significance weights to be assigned to each score. To maintain the grading scheme, the weights at each level need to sum to one. For example, the sum of weights for all the MOPs that contribute to the first sub-objective must equal one. These MOP or MOE weights indicate the relative importance of that measure to the successful accomplishment of an overall objective measurement. For a simple example with only two measures, if leaders determine that *MOP 1* is twice as important as *MOP 2* to measure *sub-objective 1*, then *MOP 1* will receive a significance weight of 0.66 and *MOP 2* will receive a significance weight of 0.34. After the weights are determined, each scaled measure is multiplied by its significance weight. The sum of weighted scores equals the score at the next level. Figure A2-6 shows an example of how these assessment scores are calculated for a sub-objective one with only two MOPs.

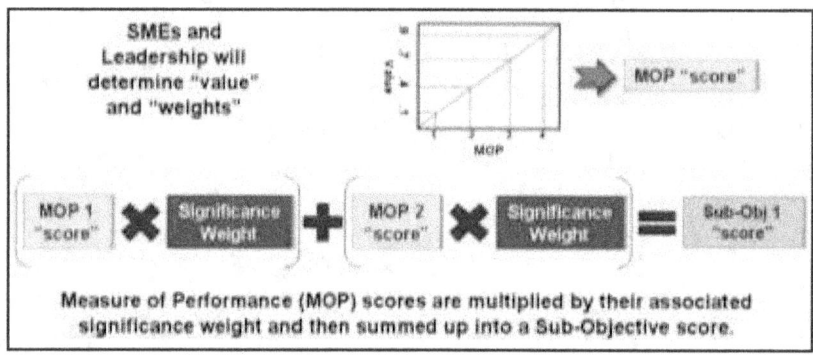

Figure A2-6: Effect Score Calculation

This process is repeated at higher levels with appropriate significance weights. Figure A2-7 illustrates that the method to calculate a *mission* score, which is analogous to the method to calculate *sub-objective* and *strategic objective* scores. That is, *sub-objective* scores are "rolled up" into a *strategic objective* score and *strategic objective* scores are "rolled up" into an overall *mission* score. A similar process is applied to the Mission Effect side of the methodology.

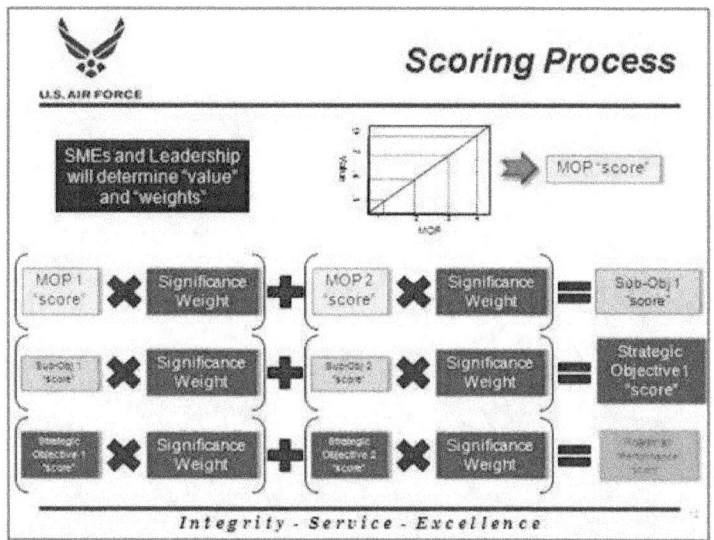

Figure A2-7: Mission Score Calculation

With each score following the grading scheme, we can also evaluate these higher scores using the grading criterion.

The assessments over time will present trends in the Air Force nuclear enterprise. After establishing a baseline, future assessment can show where improvement is occurring. The Air Force will also ensure that as it adjusts to ensure continued improvement, that follow-up AFSO21 events will be conducted to guarantee the root of all identified problems are addressed and acted on in order to measure future improvement. Using these assessments as a guide, leaders will know where to focus attention. In addition, this assessment process provides a means to reassure the Department of Defense and our national leaders on the status and trends of the Air Force nuclear enterprise.

Appendix 3 — Air Force Nuclear Enterprise Management Tool

The initial Air Force nuclear enterprise data management strategy was to capture, task, track, and archive every recommendation from every oversight report stemming from the August 2007 unauthorized nuclear weapons transfer incident. The AFNTF copied the recommendations into a spreadsheet, assigned OPRs for action, and periodically updated them to reflect current corrective action status. The recommendations were taken at face value from the reports without ever being independently validated or de-conflicted across the reports. Detailed root cause analysis was not accomplished or documented on most of the detailed studies. Only after extracting root causes, developing action plans and identifying measurable effects stemming from all the findings could a credible roadmap be drafted.

When the AFNTF conducted root cause analysis on every report finding to determine core problems and potential solutions, the need for a more robust data management tool quickly emerged. A relational database capable of correlating findings, root causes, action plans, recommendations, etc. was required to effectively capture, manage, cross-link and correlate the data.

The Air Force Nuclear Enterprise Management Tool (NEMT) has become the short-term solution. The NEMT enables the evolution from simply tracking a list of report recommendations to employing a "Strategy-to-Task" hierarchy that traces all levels of data (findings, analysis, action plans, measurements, etc.) from the Air Force nuclear enterprise (strategic level) all the way down to action plans and recommendations (tactical level) and back again. The NEMT allows users to trace the connections and interdependencies of any or all of the following levels of information within the Air Force nuclear enterprise (Figure A3-1).

- 6 Strategic Objectives

- 14 Sub-Objectives

- 136 Findings

- 57 Root Causes

- 100 Strategic Action Plans

- 200+ Action Plans

- 300+ Report Recommendations

- 250+ Nuclear Logistics Surety Team (NLST) Action Items

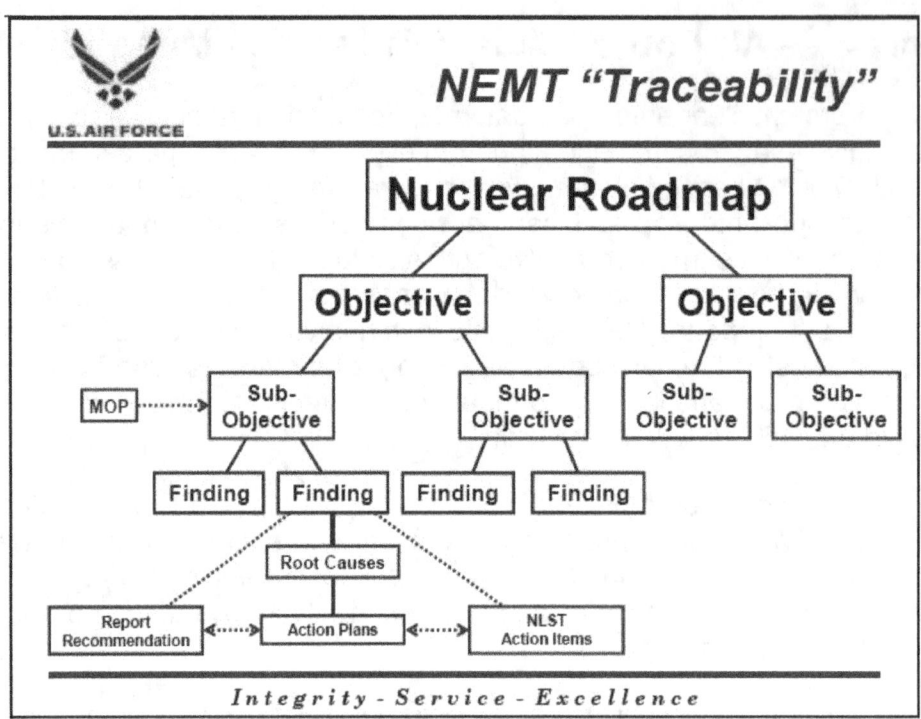

Figure A3-1: Air Force Nuclear Enterprise Management Tool Framework

The NEMT is envisioned to be hosted on the AF/A10 (AF/A3/5N) website with a web-based interface to enable OPRs the ability to provide real-time status updates and the entire community, especially Air Force senior leaders, access to current status via on-demand slides, reports, and/or queries. The NEMT will be tailored with various levels of read and write accesses, depending on the roles and responsibilities of the users.

A sample notional output of the NEMT is shown below (Figure A3-2). It provides a summary view of the overall assessment of the Air Force nuclear enterprise with respect to roadmap implementation. Also shown is a sample notional supporting slide (Figure A3-3) which provides additional details about the overall status of the six strategic objectives. Further, tailored reports and queries may be generated on any combination of data within the database.

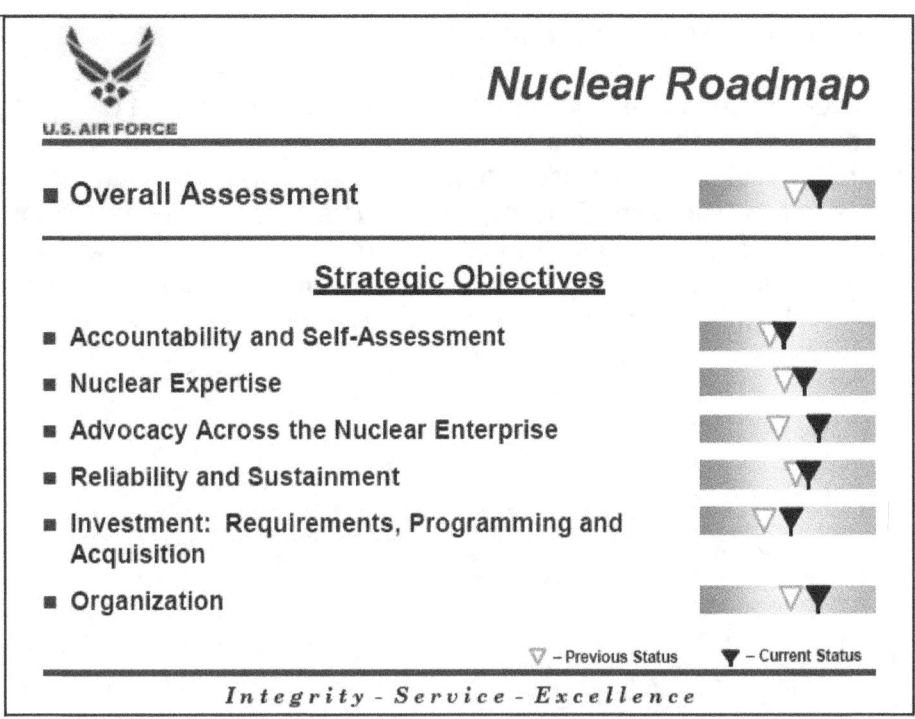

Figure A3-2: Notional Output of the NEMT Showing Overall Status

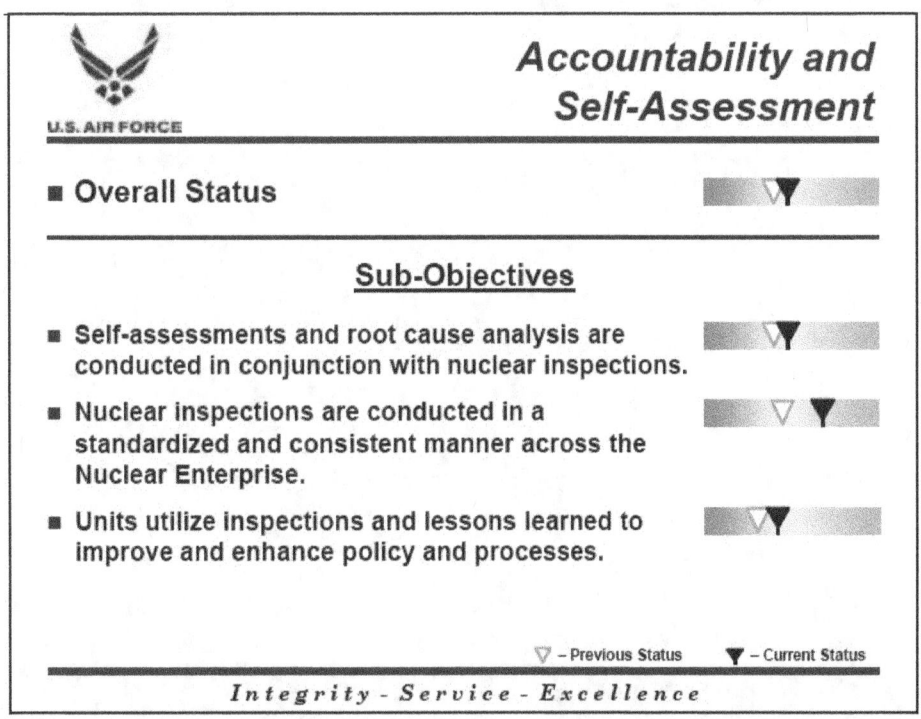

Figure A3-3: Notional NEMT Supporting Slide Showing Status of Sub-Objectives
Affecting the Overall Strategic Objective from Figure A3-2

In addition to the 6 strategic objectives, 14 sub-objectives, 136 findings, etc. that are tracked using the NEMT, there are 4 effects that provide an independent assessment of the Air Force nuclear enterprise roadmap implementation. The Directorate of Lessons Learned in Headquarters Air Force Studies, Analyses, Assessments, and Lessons Learned (AF/A9L) will provide a long-term, sustained process for the collecting, validating, disseminating and tracking these effects. The Joint Lessons Learned Information System (JLLIS) will be used to task, track, compile, and report on the effects using measures of effectiveness. Further, JLLIS can easily identify and report "observations" during implementation of the Air Force nuclear enterprise roadmap and identify those lessons not previously captured by the various reports. Additionally, the program allows easy dissemination of "best practices" throughout the national nuclear enterprise.

Appendix 4 — Report Findings

The table below contains the report findings from the Commander Directed Investigation (CDI), Blue Ribbon Review (BRR), Defense Science Board (DSB), Air Force Review and Inventory Team (AFRIT) report, Comprehensive Assessment of Nuclear Sustainment (CANS), ADM Donald Report, and Dr. Schlesinger Report.

Finding ID	Finding Text
AFRIT-01	One opportunity to enhance a critical enabler involves expanding the capability of the current enterprise information technology system used for inventory management.
AFRIT-02	Munitions Accountable Systems Officer (MASO) training represents a process enabler enhancement opportunity.
AFRIT-03	A commonly defined population of nuclear weapons-related materiel does not exist within the Department of Defense.
AFRIT-04	Not all Air Force nuclear weapons-related materiel is managed in a tightly controlled environment.
AFRIT-05	Current inventory management-related processes were characterized by a series of transactions between responsible organizations that lack an enterprise view. As a result, gaps and seams exist between and within elements of the Air Force supply chain compromising the necessary level of control and accountability for nuclear weapons-related materiel.
AFRIT-06	The Air Force inventory management system for nuclear weapons-related materiel relied on a series of legacy data systems. No single automated system existed to provide an enterprise view of Air Force managed items in all elements of the supply chain.
AFRIT-07	Responsibilities and accountabilities for enterprise-wide control of nuclear weapons-related materiel are not clearly assigned.
AFRIT-08	The experience and training of the supply chain workforce involved in the management of Air Force inventory assets requires attention at all levels.
AFRIT-09	Enlisted manpower resources for specialties involved with the storage and movement of nuclear weapons-related items is adequate. However, deployment operations tempo and planned personnel draw-downs negatively impact available manning and capability of related enlisted logistics specialties, particularly in the cargo movement career field.
AFRIT-10	Management of all nuclear weapons-related components lacks a single manager for acquisition and sustainment.
AFRIT-11	Many of the inventory overages for nuclear weapons-related components resulted due to lack of completion of demilitarization and/or disposal actions.
BRR-01	Leadership in the USAF's nuclear enterprise is professional and dedicated, but experience levels continue to decline.
BRR-02	Nuclear-related aviator experience and expertise is diminishing within the bomber and dual-capable aircraft units.

Finding ID	Finding Text
BRR-03	Intercontinental ballistic missile units find it difficult to attract and retain nuclear-experienced Airmen because of the perceived emphasis on and desirability of serving in space operations as opposed to intercontinental ballistic missile-related duties.
BRR-04	The diminishing base of nuclear experience in some support specialties makes it difficult to select and prepare leaders for command and supervisory positions.
BRR-05	USAF relationships with combatant commands for the presentation of forces are sound; however, United States Strategic Command noted some difficulty dealing with the USAF skip-echelon organizational construct.
BRR-06	Disagreement over nuclear surety inspection standardization negatively affects the relationship between the USAF and the Defense Threat Reduction Agency.
BRR-07	The USAF relationship with the OSD is strong, but there are concerns regarding USAF nuclear enterprise management.
BRR-08	The USAF nuclear enterprise is large and diverse, so direct comparison with the United States Navy nuclear organization is difficult.
BRR-09	Nuclear surety and security in the USAF are sound, but improvements can and should be made to enhance performance, particularly in light of evolving threats and the opportunities afforded by advanced technology.
BRR-10	Focus on the nuclear mission, especially in dual-capable bomber units, has diminished from the robust nuclear culture that existed during the Cold War.
BRR-11	Existing forums for integrating USAF nuclear issues exist, but these disparate groups can and should be used more effectively to serve as an enterprise-wide integrating function.
BRR-12	Nuclear surety inspection criteria are being applied differently by each major command inspection team.
BRR-13	Bomber nuclear exercises are not meeting current requirements in frequency or scale.
BRR-14	Doctrine is the cornerstone of military operations and training, but the current manual on USAF nuclear doctrine needs updating.
BRR-15	Recent DoD and USAF guidance positively changed the USAF Personnel Reliability Program, but many commanders and administrators still consider the system to be needlessly cumbersome.
BRR-16	Focus on nuclear training has shifted as a result of the increased combatant command requirements for conventional force capabilities.
BRR-17	Shortcomings exist in the training for munitions accountable systems officers, particularly on the Defense Integration and Management of Nuclear Data Services system.

Finding ID	Finding Text
BRR-18	Major commands and numbered air forces have created specific nuclear training programs that are external to the formal and institutionalized training curriculum oversight.
BRR-19	AF needs to increase opportunities for presence/influence in key nuclear billets, especially in the joint/inter-agency organizations by filling positions with highly qualified personnel.
BRR-20	Curricula at PME schools and courses devote at best only minimal time and attention to nuclear related topics.
BRR-21	The USAF is not consistently leveraging educational opportunities to optimize follow-on assignments or presence in key nuclear billets.
BRR-22	The nuclear force requires clear and detailed direction in instructions and technical orders particularly in light of a less experienced workforce, especially in aircraft units.
BRR-23	Aging transportation and handling equipment is adding to the stress on units with a nuclear mission.
BRR-24	Accountability of nuclear weapons in the USAF is sound; however, additional experience and training for munitions accountable systems officers will enhance the current process.
BRR-25	Custody and transfer processes of nuclear weapons between bases or commands are consistent; however, transfers of assets within a wing require auditable documentation.
BRR-26	Advanced technology for accountability and tracking can enhance USAF custody of nuclear assets.
BRR-27	Tracking location and status of assigned weapons and components is being accomplished using locally generated systems.
BRR-28	Potential vulnerabilities in missile field convoy operations continue to be a key concern.
BRR-29	Host nation security at overseas nuclear-capable units varies from country to country in terms of personnel, facilities, and equipment.
BRR-30	Changing and growing requirements have prompted USAF units to request nuclear security waivers.
BRR-31	To mitigate missile field security vulnerabilities, there is a critical need to fully fund a replacement helicopter and to fund the sustainment costs of the remote visual assessment.
BRR-32	Current USAF nuclear organizational construct fragments nuclear weapons advocacy and policy.
BRR-33	Manpower requirements in some nuclear-capable aircraft career fields and units may not be commensurate with total workload.
BRR-34	Program budget decision execution may have caused resource allocation weaknesses in field support for the nuclear mission.
BRR-35	Systems and equipment supporting the nuclear mission are aging and continue to impact reliability and availability.
BRR-36	Funding for second destination transportation to move nuclear weapons is inadequate.
CANS-01	A fragmented organizational structure prevented AF corporate focus across the nuclear sustainment enterprise.

Finding ID	Finding Text
CANS-02	Dispersed lines of authority contributed to a loss of systems engineering discipline within the ICBM program.
CANS-03	There is no single funding advocate for the AF nuclear sustainment enterprise.
CANS-04	There is no deliberate force development and retention management for the nuclear sustainment enterprise workforce.
CANS-05	Manpower requirements in some nuclear-capable aircraft career fields and units may not be commensurate with total workload.
CANS-06	The informal process for engineering support delays responsiveness, hinders trend analysis, and introduces unnecessary technical and programmatic risk.
CANS-07	The ICBM process for tracking completion of TCTOs is unsatisfactory.
CANS-08	The policies for DULL SWORD nuclear reporting are not clear resulting in inconsistent or random reporting.
CANS-09	There have been systemic breakdowns in the TO sustainment process.
CANS-10	The AF has not sufficiently defined nor provided governing policy for managing NWRM.
CANS-11	Logistics and supply chain management policies, procedures and processes across the nuclear enterprise are not clear, concise, nor standardized.
CANS-12	The current AF supply chain does not effectively manage or positively control NWRM.
CANS-13	Leadership does not adequately oversee nor review nuclear sustainment areas.
CANS-14	Failure to adhere to established policies coupled with multiple independent data/messaging systems cause confusion, and consume time and resources.
CANS-15	Inadequate facilities and aging equipment drive work-arounds and consume resources.
CANS-16	Nuclear policy, procedures, and processes affecting wing sustainment operations are confusing and non-standard.
CANS-17	Training required for the nuclear enterprise is inadequate.
CANS-18	AF oversight and assessment processes for nuclear sustainment activities to include inspections, LSET/MSET, and self-inspections are non-standard across the nuclear sustainment enterprise.
CANS-19	The AF failed to implement methodologies and processes for identifying systemic weaknesses and root causes.
CDI-01	Classified
CDI-02	The chain of events shows an erosion of adherence to rigid, Air Force nuclear procedures. The intricate system of nuclear checks and balances was either ignored or disregarded.
CDI-03	Numerous scheduling errors and ineffective production meetings contributed to the transfer of nuclear warheads.

Finding ID	Finding Text
CDI-04	The 2nd Operations Group did not emphasize to the flying squadrons that Combat Mission Ready-Nuclear (CMR-N) crewmembers were required for ferry sorties.
CDI-05	The ineffective production meeting procedures and lack of supervision of the scheduling process led directly to this error.
CDI-06	The Munitions Squadron supervision did not pay close attention to the schedule components.
CDI-07	The 2 OG has fundamentally changed the calculus to conventional weaponry at all levels of leadership to the core training focus.
CDI-08	The initial B-52 training course has, over time, reduced the nuclear syllabus in lieu of accomplishing conventional preparation.
CDI-09	The nuclear academia has eroded and focuses on conventional only. The B-52 Weapons Instructor Course does not teach its premier "weaponeers" the fundamentals of their nuclear trade craft.
CDI-10	The operational chain of command never read or followed the COMACC REPORD message nor was aware of the guidance in the tactical ferry book.
Donald-01	Deficient supply chain processes and noncompliance with related procedures degraded control of sensitive missile components.
Donald-02	Classified
Donald-03	Classified
Donald-04	The ICBM engineering community lacks a clear Major Command owner and has deteriorated in the exercise of technical authority.
Donald-05	Oversight, inspection, and internal audits have been ineffective in resolving recurring deficiencies.
Donald-06	The ICBM communities, including maintenance, engineering, operations, and logistic organizations, have a poorly developed self-assessment culture.
Donald-07	Changes to Air Force policies and processes degraded the level of control for sensitive missile components.
DSB-01	Over time, nuclear weapons movement procedures for bomber weapons have been compromised for expedient work processes. This evolution has occurred without adequate review and approval above the wing level.
DSB-02	There is confusion over applicability of nuclear weapons handling procedures for nuclear weapons systems that do not contain nuclear warheads.
DSB-03	The practice of storing nuclear munitions/missiles in the same facility with nuclear-training, nuclear-test, and nuclear-inert devices can lead to confusion and unnecessary access to nuclear weapons.
DSB-04	The various levels of inspection activities have failed to detect changes in process which compromised established procedure. The Nuclear Operational Readiness Inspection process requires only limited mission performance, sometimes generating as few as one aircraft.

Finding ID	Finding Text
DSB-05	While the size of the nuclear force and the deployed nuclear weapons stockpile has been greatly decreased, the complexity of the mission remains demanding. Despite these complex demands, the level of focus on the nuclear enterprise has been drastically reduced.
DSB-06	The nuclear enterprise within OSD has been dispersed and downgraded with the responsibilities of the principal office within OSD (AT&L) expanded to include chemical and biological weapons, and the nuclear enterprise within OSD (Policy) subordinated to ASD/SOLIC which has a wide-ranging portfolio.
DSB-07	With no strategic nuclear bomber forces under the operational control of the combatant command or its Air Force component and the skip echelon approach that removed 8th Air Force responsibility for B-52 operations, training, and maintenance, there was no headquarters above the wing that focused on the strategic nuclear mission.
DSB-08	The level of focus within major headquarters from Joint Staff to Air Force major command was drastically reduced with little apparent consideration or understanding of the impact such reduction across virtually all such headquarters.
DSB-08a	Daily focus on nuclear mission within the Joint Staff has been reduced to an O-6 strat operation division chief
DSB-08b	The nuclear mission within USSTRATCOM has been dispersed across 24 offices within the headquarters. The most senior officer whose daily focus is on the nuclear enterprise is an O-5 in an O-6 billet.
DSB-08c	The positions maintaining daily focus on the nuclear mission within Air Force and the Navy Staffs has been reduced to that of O-6 (Colonel/Captain).
DSB-08d	The nuclear mission within the Air Force has been dispersed from a single-focused strategic command to three operational commands that have had little or no focus on the nuclear mission. With that dispersal, the level of daily focus on the strategic nuclear bomber mission was reduced from senior flag-level to O-6 level.
DSB-09	The conventional roles of the B-52 force so dominate the nuclear role that there is minimum daily attention to the nuclear role outside the restricted area where nuclear weapons are stored and maintained. Moving nuclear weapons from where the majority of B-52 strategic bombers are based is likely to further complicate focus on the nuclear mission and further devalue the nuclear mission.
DSB-10	The B-52 initial training and advanced weapons school both largely ignore the nuclear mission. There are no flying sorties devoted to the nuclear mission in either course.
DSB-11	Over time, handling bomber nuclear weapons has come to be regarded as an exercise activity rather than a serious operational activity.

Finding ID	Finding Text
DSB-12	Public debate about the nuclear deterrent, the long-term future of nuclear weapons, approaches to sustaining the deterrent, and related subjects is inevitable and necessary as the world environment changes. There are legitimate questions about all these issues. Still, this debate cannot be allowed to obscure the most obvious and relevant facts about the nuclear enterprise. We still have a large stockpile of nuclear weapons and will almost certainly have a significant stockpile for a very long time. Those are the only facts needed to understand the need for sustained, intense attention to the nuclear enterprise and to robust nuclear weapons surety.
DSB-13	While this assessment was motivated by a specific incident of unusual magnitude, there are a large number of reports commissioned by the DoD on existing or developing concerns with the nuclear enterprise that have produced few lasting course corrections.
Schlesinger-01	Senior leadership decisions during the past 15 years have had the cumulative effect of compromising the Air Force's deterrent capabilities.
Schlesinger-02	The change in bomber mission focus away from a cadre of nuclear-experienced personnel to conventional-warfare-experienced Airmen was accompanied by a gradual decline in nuclear expertise, including in senior leadership.
Schlesinger-03	Stewardship of and focus on the policies, procedures, munitions handling processes, security, and operational exercise of nuclear weapons have been dramatically weakened.
Schlesinger-04	The decision that junior officers assigned initially to ICBMs will spend the remainder of their careers in the space mission area and thus outside the broader Air Force both devalued the mission area and had the effect of reducing the depth of Air Force nuclear experience, especially among midcareer and senior officers.
Schlesinger-05	The readiness of forces assigned to the nuclear mission has seriously eroded.
Schlesinger-06	Nuclear missions became imbedded in organizations whose primary focus is not nuclear.
Schlesinger-07	Overwhelming emphasis was given to conventional operations.
Schlesinger-08	The grade levels of line and staff appointments of those whose daily business involved nuclear weapons were lowered.
Schlesinger-09	The nuclear mission and those who performed it were generally devalued.
Schlesinger-10	There was no single command to advocate for the resources required to support nuclear capabilities. Collectively this meant that no one Command in the Air Force had "ownership" of the nuclear mission.

Finding ID	Finding Text
Schlesinger-11	The New Triad concept in National and Defense policy documents is not generally understood by many of those involved in the Air Force nuclear mission. This lack of clarity is sensed all the way down to the crew level. In addition, the Air Force has not updated its doctrine on nuclear deterrence since 1998.
Schlesinger-12	Lacking a complete understanding of the importance of the nuclear mission, the Air Force has experienced instances where personnel have failed to maintain discipline in following procedures, and some airmen do not view the nuclear mission as vital.
Schlesinger-13	Air Force leaders have failed to support appropriate resource allocation for the nuclear deterrence mission. As a result, mission readiness has been significantly degraded.
Schlesinger-14	Air Force leaders failed in their leadership responsibilities to shift priorities and adjust policies and resources in ways needed to maintain robust nuclear stewardship, resulting in the inattention that led to the Minot-Barksdale and Taiwan incidents.
Schlesinger-15	The Air Force has failed to establish adequate procedures and technical orders related to nuclear operations and support. Air Force streamlining efforts and personnel reduction and allocation decisions have led to significant degradation in the nuclear mission.
Schlesinger-16	Inspection processes are not standardized across major commands, inspectors are not appropriately trained and inspections are not sufficiently comprehensive and frequent.
Schlesinger-17	The Air Force nuclear exercise program has been marked by infrequency and low levels of unit participation.
Schlesinger-18	The Air Force needs to focus on developing and managing nuclear-experienced personnel, particularly in maintenance and security personnel. A bias exists in promotion boards against airmen in nuclear-related fields.
Schlesinger-19	The concept of nuclear deterrence and the role of nuclear weapons in current circumstances have fallen out of the core military doctrine taught in the Air Force PME.
Schlesinger-20	Today no senior leader in the USAF "owns" the nuclear mission. The current organization is not properly structured to meet requirements.
Schlesinger-21	Bomber and ICBM forces today suffer from manpower shortages in numerous areas.
Schlesinger-22	There is inadequate equipment for training.
Schlesinger-23	Support and handling infrastructure require new funding for modernization and sustainability.
Schlesinger-24	In the past decade, no-notice inspections have been almost entirely replaced by those carried out according to a published schedule.
Schlesinger-25	Air Force inspection teams tend to lack the organic wherewithal to conduct effective nuclear inspection activities.
Schlesinger-26	The Staff Assistance (SAV) program is underused, under resourced, and in need of guidance.

Finding ID	Finding Text
Schlesinger-27	"Skip echelon" arrangements (from Wing to MAJCOM without going through the NAF staff) have undermined NAF leadership's sense of responsibility and accountability for its subordinate units.
Schlesinger-28	GDF changes do not fully address the numbers of bombers available for training and test purposes, which may divert combat-coded aircraft for these purposes.
Schlesinger-29	Unit Manning Documents are not universally coded to identify key nuclear billets for those positions deemed critical for a unit to conduct its nuclear missions.
Schlesinger-30	Current Air Force organizational practices and readiness status do not satisfy the national security need for a bomber force that is credible, visible, and responsive to the nuclear deterrent role.
Schlesinger-31	ACC has been strained to support Combatant Command demands of the past decade and a half to provide conventional forces to support joint operations.
Schlesinger-32	The headquarters of Commander, 8th Air Force is inadequately manned to manage a significant span of control.
Schlesinger-33	An officer completing a standard four-year tour as a missileer, while well steeped in ICBM nuclear operations, has limited intermediate rank opportunity in the missile career field…The result has been a fairly rich mix of middle grade officers in the space specialty, but a correspondingly leaner number of experienced missileers, especially in the field grand ranks.
Schlesinger-34	AFPC can assign the individual based on the volunteer statement, usually for a one year tour, without the supervisor's or commander's knowledge or approval.
Schlesinger-35	AFPC provide no backfill for the volunteer until the volunteer's overseas tour is completed, often 12 months long.
Schlesinger-36	Rarely do unit personnel receive current intelligence relative to their nuclear mission.

Appendix 5 — Development of the Air Force Nuclear Weapons Security Roadmap

Introduction

The top priority of the AF is reinvigorating the nuclear enterprise. To achieve this goal we must effectively secure, maintain, operate, and sustain our Nation's nuclear capabilities. To properly address security, the Deputy Chief of Staff, Logistics, Installations and Mission Support (AF/A4/7) chartered the Air Force Security Forces (SF) to develop the *Air Force Nuclear Weapons Security Roadmap 2010.* Functional experts from the Air Staff, Air Force Major Commands (MAJCOMs), Sandia National Laboratory (SNL), Science Applications International Corporation (SAIC) and field agency nuclear communities met to initiate/complete the nuclear weapons security roadmap process.

The purpose of the Air Force Nuclear Weapons Security (NWS) Roadmap is to present the vision for sustaining Air Force nuclear security, and provide a detailed way ahead through continued refinement and enhancement in order to meet the intent of *National Security Presidential Directive-28.* The Air Force NWS Roadmap is a separate but contributing effort to the *Reinvigorating the Air Force Nuclear Enterprise Roadmap.*

The data gathered for the NWS Roadmap ensures effective readiness of our nuclear security forces, and provides a key source document for the Department of Defense (DoD) and the Air Force regarding current Air Force nuclear security requirements, plans, and programs. In particular, the security roadmap presents the Air Force SF strategy for the future.

Risk to our nuclear weapons will never be eliminated; however the NWS Roadmap strives to reduce risk wherever possible. The focus of this process was to gain needed insight from nuclear security, intelligence, and use control experts on the vulnerability, threat, and consequence of an attack to US nuclear weapons under Air Force control in a variety of configurations and environments. The data collected was factored into the risk model to determine *relative* risk between different nuclear security environments.

The Air Force NWS Roadmap has two major objectives. The first is to further synchronize the nuclear security roadmaps of the Air Force MAJCOMs with the Air Force as a whole, and effectively integrate operations, maintenance, active and passive defenses, use control, weapons design and intelligence to ensure security standards are met. To accomplish, it will be necessary to invest additional resources to close the desired capability gaps and mitigate security shortfalls. The second objective of the Air Force Nuclear Weapons Security Roadmap is to develop a tool for determining a comprehensive and analytically-based investment strategy for the most pressing nuclear weapons security needs. The analytical foundation provided by the relative risk model can strengthen the arguments for nuclear security requirements and enable the security community to better compete for scarce resources in the Air Force corporate process.

The Air Force NWS Roadmap is part of an on-going process in analyzing nuclear security vulnerabilities (capability gaps and shortfalls) and the effect of various mitigation measures. As the Air Force nuclear community gains experience with the risk methodology, refines and refreshes the input data, and develops additional risk reduction options, it will continue to be used to update the assessment. Particularly valuable will be more definitive data on the effectiveness of current and projected technologies and materiel solutions. Further iterations of the model will provide updated information on the resulting effect on vulnerability of various options and how each component of the model can be considered in the overall risk reduction effort. Additionally, further refinement of the relative risk model could include factoring localized threat assessments into the analysis.

Background and History

An attempt to produce a nuclear weapons security roadmap was made in 2005. This effort hypothesized how the Air Force nuclear MAJCOMs *could* achieve denial capability by the 2018 time frame through potential manpower increases; upgrades to facilities, equipment, and security systems; training reforms; and through changes to tactics, techniques, and procedures (TTPs). It was later re-designated a program of record (POR) by retaining the programmed elements and discarding the hypothetical elements. The POR did not, however, effectively integrate the MAJCOM security roadmaps into an overall Air Force strategy for nuclear weapons security. Additionally, the POR was not based on risk reduction, nor did it have an investment strategy.

Air Force Nuclear Security Risk Model

The concept of risk is fundamental to making sound decisions regarding security of critical assets when there is uncertainty surrounding the timing, nature, scope and success of potential threats. It is also a fundamental consideration when making investment decisions and tradeoffs in a fiscally constrained environment. While our nuclear assets will never be free from risk, an analytic process ensures we strive to reduce risk across all environments.

For Air Force nuclear weapons security, relative risk is a function of the vulnerability of a given target containing one or more nuclear weapons, the consequence of failure if an attack on the weapon(s) occurs, and the probability of an attack occurring. It is important to note the use of the term *relative*. Risk is never zero, and as it is discussed and used in this report, it does not have an *absolute value* -- only a *relative* one to other operational environments.

The input for each component of the model is derived from qualitative and quantitative data. The probability of attack and consequences of failure data were taken from previous studies and year long processes with AF/A3S, AF/A2, and SAF/IGX to develop this risk approach. The nuclear weapons security SMEs considered these components independently of one another, and each was weighted equally.

Nuclear Security Analysis of Alternatives

Sandia National Labs prepared an Analysis of Alternatives (AoA) for the Air Force on behalf of Headquarters AF/A7S. This AoA complements and supports the efforts of the

NWS to improve and synchronize the nuclear security roadmaps for the MAJCOMs and the Air Force as a whole. The overall process improves the effective management and prioritization of limited resources to reduce the risk associated with Air Force nuclear weapons to the greatest extent practical.

While the AoA is essentially a cost versus performance analysis, it also provides a level of detail to address the most critical vulnerabilities with systematic and performance-based solutions. The primary purpose of the AoA is to identify solutions and complementary solution sets that provide the greatest risk reduction in the most critical environments.

The AoA supports the Air Force investment strategy and POM efforts by evaluating data, including relative risk and vulnerability for each environment, and the relative contribution of risk by attack type, condition, and other factors. SNL used information from current MAJCOM roadmaps, existing data and analyses, and discussions with Air Force personnel and SNL SMEs to prepare the AoA.

Sandia National Labs staff prepared an estimate of the system performance and cost for each upgrade set. This cost versus benefit analysis demonstrated, at a high level, the optimal approach for each environment. This evaluation followed the SNL developed methodology for evaluating physical protection systems for critical and high-value assets. The SNL risk and performance evaluation process has been used for more than 30 years, and is recognized, accepted, and well understood in the broad security community, including the Department of Defense, the Department of Energy, and Department of Homeland Security. When quantitative data is used, the equations generate quantifiable results.

Summary

The top priority of the AF is reinvigorating the nuclear enterprise. A key contributor to the nuclear enterprise is security. The AF NWS Roadmap will identify and implement the most cost-effective security performance improvements. The Air Force Nuclear Weapons Security Roadmap provides a living document to maintain a secure nuclear stockpile and supporting infrastructure through a fiscally responsible manner. It directly contributes to the reinvigoration of the Air Force nuclear enterprise.

Appendix 6 — Acronyms

ACC	Air Combat Command
ADCON	Administrative Control
ADM	Admiral
ADP	Airmen Development Plan
AE	Aeromedical Evacuation
AETC	Air Education and Training Command
AF	Air Force
AF/A1	Air Force Manpower, Personnel, and Services
AF/A3/5	Air Force Operations, Plans, and Requirements
AF/A3/5N	Air Force Operations, Plans, and Requirements Nuclear (now AF/A10)
AF/A4/7	Air Force Logistics, Installations, and Mission Support
AF/A8	Air Force Strategic Plans and Procedures
AF/A9	Air Force Studies & Analyses, Assessments, and Lessons Learned
AF/A10	Air Force Nuclear Operations, Plans, and Requirements (previously AF/A3/5N)
AF/CV	Vice Air Force Chief of Staff
AF/SE	Air Force Safety
AF/SEW	Air Force Safety Weapons
AF/SG	Air Force Surgeon General
AF/TE	Air Force Test and Evaluation
AFB	Air Force Base
AFCS	Air Force Corporate Structure
AFGSC	Air Force Global Strike Command
AFI	Air Force Instruction

AFIA	Air Force Inspection Agency
AFMAN	Air Force Manual
AFMC	Air Force Materiel Command
AFNGOSG	Air Force Nuclear General Officer Steering Group
AFNTF	Air Force Nuclear Task Force
AFNWC	Air Force Nuclear Weapons Center
AFR	Air Force Regulation
AFRIT	Air Force Review and Inventory Team
AFSC	Air Force Specialty Code
AFSO 21	Air Force Smart Operations for the 21st Century
AFSPC	Air Force Space Command
AFSTRAT	Air Forces Strategic Command
AF/TE	Air Force Test and Evaluation
AFTO	Air Force Technical Order
AIT	Automatic Identification Technology
ALC	Air Logistics Center
ALCM	Air Launched Cruise Missile
AMC	Air Mobility Command
AoA	Analysis of Alternatives
AOR	Area of Responsibility
APPG	Annual Planning and Programming Guidance
AU	Air University
BRAC	Base Realignment and Closure
BRR	Blue Ribbon Review
C4ISR	Command, Control, Communications, Computers and Intelligence, Surveillance, and Reconnaissance

CANS	Comprehensive Assessment of Nuclear Sustainment
CAS	Close Air Support
CBRN	Chemical, Biological, Radiological, and Nuclear
CC	Commander
CCDE	Command and Control Display Equipment
CCM	Capability and Credibility Model
CDC	Career Development Course
CDI	Commander Directed Investigation
CDP	Civilian Development Plan
CDR	Commander
CENTCOM	Central Command
CF	Comprehensive Findings
CFETP	Career Field Education and Training Plan
CFM	Career Field Manager
CJCSI	Chairman Joint Chiefs of Staff Instruction
COA	Course of Action
COCOM	Combatant Command
CONEMP	Concept of Employment
CONOPS	Concept of Operations
CONUS	Continental United States
CPI	Continuous Process Improvement
CSAF	Chief of Staff, United States Air Force
DCA	Dual-Capable Aircraft
DCR	DOTMLPF Change Recommendation
DCS	Deputy Chief of Staff
DIAMONDS	Defense Integration and Management of Nuclear Data Services

DLA	Defense Logistics Agency
DMS	Defense Message System
DOC	Designed Operational Capability
DoD	Department of Defense
DOE	Department of Energy
DOTMLPF	Doctrine, Organization, Training, Materiel, Leadership and Education, Personnel, and Facilities
DPAS	Defense Priorities and Allocations System
DRU	Direct Reporting Unit
DSB	Defense Science Board
DTRA	Defense Threat Reduction Agency
EBAO	Effects-Based Approach to Operations
ECSS	Expeditionary Combat Support System
EDP	Enlisted Development Plan
EET	Exercise Evaluation Team
ESC	Electronic Systems Center
ETARS	Electronic Technical Assistance Requests
ETIC	Estimated Time of Completion
EW	Electronic Warfare
FMDC	Force Management and Development Council
FOC	Full Operational Capability
FTAC	First Term Airman's Center
FTU	Formal Training Unit
FTX	Field Training Exercise
FY	Fiscal Year
FYDP	Future Year Defense Program

GO	General Officer
GWOT	Global War on Terrorism
HAF	Headquarters Air Force
HQ	Headquarters
ICBM	Intercontinental Ballistic Missile
ICBMSG	Intercontinental Ballistic Missile Systems Group
IG	Inspector General
IGEMS	IG Evaluation Management System
IMDS	Integrated Maintenance Data System
IMT	Information Management Tool
INRAD	Intrinsic Radiation
INSI	Initial Nuclear Surety Inspection
IOC	Initial Operational Capability
IPT	Integrated Process Team
ISR	Intelligence, Surveillance, and Reconnaissance
IT	Information Technology
JFCC	Joint Functional Component Command
JLLIS	Joint Lessons Learned Information System
JROC	Joint Requirements Oversight Council
LCOM	Logistics Composite Model
LRU	Line Replacement Unit
LSET	Logistics Standardization and Evaluation Team
MAJCOM	Major Command
MAJCOM/CV	Major Command Vice Commander
MASO	Munitions Accountable Systems Officer
MMXG	Missile Maintenance Group

MOE	Measures of Effectiveness
MOP	Measures of Performance
MSET	Maintenance Standardization and Evaluation Team
MUNS	Munitions Squadron
MUNSS	Munitions Support Squadron
NAF	Numbered Air Force
NAF/CC	Numbered Air Force Commander
NATO	North American Treaty Organization
NCE	Nuclear Capabilities Exercise
NEAP	Nuclear Enterprise Advisory Panel
NEMT	Nuclear Enterprise Management Tool
NLTFP	National Laboratory Technical Fellowship Program
NLST	Nuclear Logistics Surety Team
NMOC	Nuclear Munitions Officer Course
NMS	National Military Strategy
NNSA	National Nuclear Security Administration
NOC	NSPD-28 Oversight Committee
NORI	Nuclear Operational Readiness Inspection
NPR	Nuclear Posture Review
NSAV	Nuclear Staff Assistance Visit
NSI	Nuclear Surety Inspection
NSN	National Stock Number
NSSAV	Nuclear Surety Staff Assistance Visit
NWRM	Nuclear Weapons-Related Materiel
NWS	Nuclear Weapons Security
NWSSG	Nuclear Weapons System Safety Group

OCONUS	Outside the Continental United States
OCR	Office of Coordinating Authority
ODP	Officer Development Plan
OEF	Operation Enduring Freedom
OIF	Operation Iraqi Freedom
OODA	Observe, Orient, Decide, and Act
OPLAN	Operation Plan
OPR	Office of Primary Responsibility
OPSEC	Operational Security
OPSTEMPO	Operational Tempo
OSD	Office Secretary of Defense
OSD/AT&L	Office Secretary of Defense, Acquisition, Technology, and Logistics
OSS&E	Operational Safety, Suitability, and Effectiveness
PACAF	Pacific Air Forces
PAD	Program Action Directive
PBD	Program Budget Decision
PE	Program Element
PEM	Program Element Manager
PEO	Program Executive Officer
PIC	Positive Inventory Control
PME	Professional Military Education
PMR	Program Management Review
PNAF	Primary Nuclear Airlift Force
POM	Program Objective Memorandum
POR	Program of Record
P-Plan	Programming Plan

PPBE	Planning, Programming, Budgeting, and Execution
PRP	Personnel Reliability Program
QA	Quality Assurance
QDR	Quadrennial Defense Review
RCA	Root Cause Analysis
RLA	Repair Level Analysis
RSTS	Re-entry System Test Set
RWT	Realistic Weapons Trainers
S-FRD	Secret-Formerly Restricted Data
SAC	Strategic Air Command
SAF	Secretary of the Air Force
SAF/AQ	Assistant Secretary of the Air Force, Acquisition
SAF/AQP	Assistant Secretary of the Air Force, Acquisitions, Global Power
SAF/CM	Secretary of the Air Force Strategic Communications
SAF/IG	Secretary of the Air Force Inspector General
SAF/LL	Secretary of the Air Force Legislative Liaison
SAF/SO	Secretary of the Air Force's Smart Operations
SAF/US	Under Secretary of the Air Force
SAF/USA	Secretary of the Air Force Space Acquisitions
SAIC	Science Applications International Corporation
SAV	Staff Assistance Visit
SBSS	Standard Base Supply System
SCM	Supply Chain Management
SecAF	Secretary of the Air Force
SECDEF	Secretary of Defense
SES	Senior Executive Service

SF	Security Forces
SIPRNet	Secret Internet Protocol Router Network
SME	Subject Matter Expert
SNL	Sandia National Laboratory
SORTS	Status of Resources and Training Systems
SSP	Strategic Systems Program
TIG	The Inspector General
T.O.	Technical Order
TP	Technical Procedure
TRAC	Threat Reduction Advisory Committee
TTP	Tactics Techniques Procedures
U&TW	Utilization and Training Workshop
UAS	Unmanned Aerial System
UCP	Unified Command Plan
UK	United Kingdom
URL	Unfunded Requirements List
US	United States
USAF	United States Air Force
USAFE	United States Air Forces Europe
USC	United States Code
USN	United States Navy
USSTRATCOM	United States Strategic Command
vMFP	Virtual Major Force Program
WIC	Weapons Instructor Course
WIP	Weapon Integration Plan
WMD	Weapons of Mass Destruction

WS3	Weapon Storage and Security Systems
WSA	Weapons Storage Area
WSR	Weapon System Reliability
WSSR	Weapon System Safety Rule

Appendix 7 — References

REPORTS

Report of the *Defense Science Board Task Force on Future Strategic Strike Forces*, 2004

Strategic Capabilities Assessment - 2004 (S//FRD//NF)

Report of the *Defense Science Board Task Force on Nuclear Capabilities Report Summary*, 2006

Commander Directed Report of Investigation Concerning an Unauthorized Transfer of Nuclear Warheads Between Minot AFB, North Dakota and Barksdale AFB, Louisiana - 30 August 2007 (S//FRD//MR)

Air Force Blue Ribbon Review (BRR) of Nuclear Weapons Policies and Procedures, 8 February 2008

The Defense Science Board (DSB) Permanent Task Force on Nuclear Weapons Surety – Report on Unauthorized Movement of Nuclear Weapons (Gen Welch), February 2008 (Revised April 2008)

NSS Oversight of USAF Nuclear Surety Inspections, 1 April 2008

Investigation into the Shipment of Sensitive Missile Components to Taiwan (ADM Donald Report) - 22 May 2008 (S//FRD//NOFORN)

Air Force Inventory and Assessment: Nuclear Weapons and Nuclear Weapons-Related Materiel, 25 May 2008

Air Force Comprehensive Assessment of Nuclear Sustainment (CANS) - July 2008 (S//FRD//NOFORN)

SECDEF Task Force on DoD Nuclear Weapons Management (Dr Schlesinger), September 2008 (T)

NATIONAL STRATEGIES

The National Security Strategy of the United States of America, March 2006

National Defense Strategy of the United States of America (NDS), June 2008

National Military Strategy of the United States of America (NMS), 2004

The National Military Strategy to Combat Weapons of Mass Destruction, 13 February 2006

NATIONAL DIRECTIVES

National Security Presidential Directive-3, 15 February 2001 (S)

National Security Presidential Directive-4, 15 February 2001 (S)

National Security Presidential Directive-10, *U.S. Strategic Nuclear Force*, 21 December 2001 (S)

National Security Presidential Directive-28, *United States Nuclear Weapons Command and Control, Safety, and Security*, 20 June 2003 (S)

National Security Presidential Directive-35, *Nuclear Weapons Deployment Authorization*, 6 May 2004 (S//FRD)

Presidential Initiative on Nuclear Arms, 27 September 1991

Presidential Nuclear Initiative II, 28 January 1992

The Alliance's Strategic Concept, April 1999

Fiscal Year 2005 Joint Surety Report, IAW NSPD-28 - 2005 (S//FRD)

DEPARTMENT OF DEFENSE

DoD Publication, Quadrennial Defense Review Report, Office of the Secretary of Defense, February 2006

Department of Defense Directive S-5210.81, *United States Nuclear Weapons Command, Control, Safety, and Security*, 2005 (S)

Department of Defense Directive 0-5 100.30, *Department of Defense Command and Control*, 2006

Department of Defense S-5210-41-MIAir Force Manual 3 1-108, *Nuclear Weapon Security Manual*, 2007 (S//NF)

Department of Defense Directive 5210.42, *Personnel Reliability Program*, 2001

Department of Defense Directive 5230.16, *Nuclear Accident and Incident Public Affairs (PA) Guidance*, 1993

T.O. 11N-25-1, *DoD Nuclear Weapons Technical Inspection System*

JOINT SERVICES

CJCSI 3260.01A, *Joint Policy Governing Positive Control Material and Devices*, 2002 (S//FRD)

CJCSI 3 110.04-B, *Nuclear Supplement to Joint Strategic Capabilities Plan* (TS)

Policy Guidance for the Employment of Nuclear Weapons (NUWEP) (TS)

Unified Command Plan (draft), 8 August 2008

Nuclear Response CONOPS, version 9, 11 October 2006 (S//20140428)

Integrated Operations Directive (IOD) A, *Guidance for Global Deterrence Force Operation*, 1 Jul 2008 (S)

Joint Publication (JP) 1; *Doctrine for the Armed Forces of the United States*, 14 May 2007

JP 1-02, *Department of Defense Dictionary of Military and Associated Terms*, 12 April 2001 (as amended through March 2004)

JP 3-12, *Doctrine for Joint Nuclear Operations*, Final Coordination (2), 15 March 2005

Joint Vision 2020, June 2000

Joint Air Tasking Order Processes (JATOPC) Course; *Student Guide Book 1*, February 2004

Deterrence Operations Joint Operating Concept; Version 2.0, December 2006

Irregular Warfare (IW) Joint Operating Concept (JOC), Version 1.0, 11 September 2007

Joint Logistics (Distribution) Joint Integrating Concept Version 1.0, 7 February 2006

Seabasing, Joint Integrating Concept, v1, 1 August 2005

Department of Defense Homeland Defense and Civil Support Joint Operating Concept Version 2.0, 1 October 2007

Force Management Joint Functional Concept Version 1.0, 2 June 2005

Joint Integrating Concept Final Version 1.0, 1 Sep 2005

Joint Integrating Concept for Combating Weapons of Mass Destruction Version 1.0, 10 December 2007

Joint Training Functional Concept Version 1.0, 14 August 2007

Joint Urban Operations Joint Integrating Concept Version 1.0, 23 July 2007

Global Strike Joint Integrating Concept, v1, 10 January 2005

Persistent Intelligence, Surveillance, and Reconnaissance: Planning and Direction, Joint Integrating Concept, v1, 29 March 2007

Deterrence Operations Joint Operating Concept, Version 2.0, December 2006

Seabasing, Joint Integrating Concept, v1, 1 August 2005

JROC Functional Concept for Battlespace Awareness, 31 December 2003

JROC Joint Command and Control Functional Concept, February 2004

JROC Force Application Functional Concept, 5 March 2004

JROC Focused Logistics Joint Functional Concept, Version 1.0, December 2003

JROC Protection Joint Functional Concept, Version 1.0, 30 June 2004

JROC Functional Concept for Battlespace Awareness, 31 December 2003

JROC Joint Command and Control Functional Concept, February 2004

JROC Force Application Functional Concept, 5 March 2004

JROC Focused Logistics Joint Functional Concept, Version 1.0, December 2003

JROC Protection Joint Functional Concept, Version 1.0, 30 June 2004

Major Combat Operations Joint Operating Concept, Version 2.0, December 2006

Capstone Concept for Joint Operations, Version 2.0, August 2005

Net-Centric Environment Joint Functional Concept, Version 1.0, 7 April 2005

Net-Centric Operational Environment Joint Integrating Concept, Version 1.0, 31 October 2005

Military Support to Stabilization, Security, Transition, and Reconstruction Operations Joint Operating Concept Version 2.0, December 2006

USSTRATCOM

USSTRATCOM ICBM and Bomber Strategic Employment Requirements, 30 July 2007 (S//FRD)

USSTRATCOM Operational Plan (OPLAN) 8010-08, Global Deterrence and Strike, 1 February 2008 (S)

AIR FORCE

SecAF MEMO, *Rebuilding the Nuclear Enterprise*, 26 June 2008

VCSAF Memo, *Air Force Nuclear Task Force*, no date

2007 US Air Force Posture Statement

Program Budget Decision (PBD) 720 Air Force Transformation Flight Plan, 20 December 2005

Program Budget Decision (PBD) 725 (USSTRATCOM TRIAD)

Air Force Vision 2020, Global Vigilance, Reach, and Power, 2002

AFDD 1, *Air Force Basic Doctrine*, 17 November 2003

AFDD 1-1, *Leadership and Force Development*, 18 February 2006

AFDD 2, *Organization and Employment of Aerospace Power*, 17 February 2000

AFDD 2-1.5, *Nuclear Operations*, 15 July 1998

AFDD 2-1.2, *Strategic Attack*, 12 June 2007

AFDD 2-1.8, *Counter-Chemical, Biological, Radiological and Nuclear Operations*, 26 January 2007

AFPD 91-1, *Nuclear Weapons and Systems Surety*, 13 February 2007

AFI 21-101, *Aircraft and Equipment Maintenance Management*, 29 June 2006

AFI 36-2640, *Total Force Development* (Active duty Officer) Volume 1, 23 January 2004

AFI 90-201, *Inspector General Activities*, 22 November 2004

AFI 91-101, *Air Force Nuclear Weapons Surety Program*, 19 December 2005

AFI 91-108, *Air Force Nuclear Weapons Intrinsic Radiation Safety Program*, 29 November 1993

AFI 91-111, *Safety Rules for US Strategic Bomber Aircraft*, 14 February 2006

AFMAN 91-221, *Weapons Safety Investigations and Reports*, 18 June 2004

AFMAN 10-3902, *Nuclear Weapons Personnel Reliability Program*, 13 November 2006 (supplement to DOD)

ACCI 91-109, *Nuclear Surety Staff Assistance Visit Program and Responsibilities*, 25 May 2006

AFSO21 Playbook

509 BW Nuclear Operations Review – Policy Memorandum, 11 July 2008

ACC Nuclear Operations Memorandum, 24 June 2008

Graybeard Panel Report, August 2008

Transition of the B-52 Bomber from SAC to ACC: A Case Study of Transformation, *Major Tyrell A. Chamberlain, USAF, June 2006*

8 AF/CC briefing, *SecAF Nuclear Deterrence Briefing*, 1 July 2008

CAF/MAF Commander's Conference briefing, *Nuclear Deterrence Operations*, 2008

Background Paper on Global Deterrence Force, HAF v1, July 2008

NAVY

Naval Power 21 ... A Naval Vision, October 2002

Sea Power 21 Projecting Decisive Joint Capabilities, Adm Vern Clark, US Navy Proceedings, October 2002

Naval Doctrine Publication 1 *Naval Warfare*, 28 March 1994

Navy Strategic Systems Programs Program Overview Presentation, December 2007

REPORTS TO CONGRESS

GAO-08-1032T Report: *NUCLEAR WEAPONS Views on NNSA's Proposal to Transform the Nuclear Weapons Complex*, 17 July 2008

Nuclear Posture Review, December 2001 (S//FRD//NF)

Nuclear Posture Review: Implementation Plan, March 2003 (S//FRD//NF)

TREATIES AND AGREEMENTS

African Nuclear Weapon Free Zone Treaty (The Treaty of Pelindaba)

Agreement Between the United States of America and the Union of Soviet Socialist Republics on the Prevention of Nuclear War, 22 June 1973

Convention on the Physical Protection of Nuclear Material, 8 February 1987

Comprehensive Test Ban Treaty

International Atomic Energy Agency Additional Protocol

Agreement Between the United States of America and the International Atomic Energy Agency for the Application of Safeguards in the United States, 31 December 1980

Non-Traditional Strike Final Report, 26 September 2007

Treaty Between the United States of America and the Union of Soviet Socialist Republics on the Elimination of Intermediate-Range and Shorter-Range Missiles (INF Treaty), 27 December 1988

National Security and Nuclear Weapons in the 21" Century, March 2008 (S//FRD)

Treaty Banning Nuclear Weapon Tests in the Atmosphere, in Outer Space, and Under Water (Limited Test Ban Treaty), 10 October 1963

Treaty Between the United States of America and the Russian Federation on Strategic Offensive Reductions (Moscow Treaty), 24 May 2002

Treaty of Mutual Cooperation and Security Treaty Between Japan and the United States of America, 19 January 1960

Mutual Defense Treaty between the Republic of Korea and the United States of America, 17 November 1954

Treaty on the Nonproliferation of Nuclear Weapons, 5 March 1970

Treaty on Principles Governing the Activities of States in the Exploration and Use of Outer Space, Including the Moon and other Celestial Bodies (Outer Space Treaty), 10 October 1967

Treaty on the Prohibition of the Emplacement of Nuclear Weapons and Other Weapons of Mass Destruction on the Seabed and the Ocean Floor and in the Subsoil Thereof (Seabed Arms Control Treaty), 18 May 1972

South Pacific Nuclear Weapon Free Zone Treaty, 6 August 1985

Treaty on the Southeast Asia Nuclear Weapon Free Zone, 27 March 1997

Treaty between the United States of America and the Union of Soviet Socialist Republics on the Reduction and Limitation of Strategic Offensive Arms (START Treaty), 31 July 1991

The Antarctic Treaty, 23 June 1961

The North Atlantic Treaty, 4 April 1949

Treaty for the Prohibition of Nuclear Weapons in Latin America, 22 April 1968

Treaty between the United States of America and the Union of Soviet Socialist Republics on Underground Nuclear Explosions for Peaceful Purposes, 11 December 1990

Treaty Between the United States of America and the Union of Soviet Socialist Republics on the Limitation of Underground Nuclear Weapon Testing (Threshold Test Ban Treaty), 11 December 1990

Agreement between the Government of the United Kingdom of Great Britain and Northern Ireland and the Government of the United States of America for Cooperation on the uses of Atomic Energy for Mutual Defence Purposes (UK - US Mutual Defense Treaty), 4 August 1958; with Amendments/ 23A. 2004 Amendment to the UK - US Mutual Defense Treaty / 23B. UK - US Exchange of Letters

Taiwan Relations Act, 1979

Joint Statement of the US Japan Security Consultative Commission, 1 May 2007

Joint Communiqué 2006 US Korea, 20 October 2006

OTHER

Can Deterrence Be Tailored? M. Elaine Bunn, Strategic Forum, National Defense University, Institute for National Strategic Studies, No. 225, January 2007

Center for Strategic International Studies, *The Department of Defense and the Nuclear Mission in the 21st Century A Beyond Goldwater-Nichols Phase 4 Report*, March 2008

The Future of the United Kingdom's Nuclear Deterrent, Presented to Parliament by The Secretary of State for Foreign and Commonwealth Affairs By Command of Her Majesty, December 2006

Keeney, Ralph L., *Value-Focused Thinking: A Path to Creative Decision-making*, Harvard University Press, Cambridge, Massachusetts, 1992

Sagan, Scott D. *The Limits of Safety,* Princeton, NJ: Princeton University Press,1993

Appendix 8 — Air Force Nuclear Task Force Members

Leadership

Maj Gen C. Donald Alston, AF/A3/5N, Chair

Maj Gen (ret) Charles Henderson, AF/A3/5N, Deputy Chair

Dr. Billy Mullins, AF/A3/5N, Deputy Chair

Col Jeffrey Kindley, AF/A3/5N-R, Chief Strategy Cell

Lt Col Tyrell Chamberlain, 2BW/SE, Deputy Chief Strategy Cell

Col Gregory Boyette, AF/A5RS, Chief Integration Cell

Lt Col Lloyd Ringgold, AF/A3/5N-O, Deputy Chief Integration Cell

Col Michael Shoults, AF/A3/5N-P, Organizational Development Cell

GreyBeards

Maj Gen (ret) Thomas H. Neary, Chair

VADM (ret) James W. Metzger

Maj Gen (ret) Kenneth L. Hageman Sr.

Maj Gen (ret) Gregory H. Power

Maj Gen (ret) Robert L. Smolen

Dr. Theodore Hardebeck

Col (ret) Larry S. Chandler

Core Team Members

Lt Col Scott Boushell, SAF/XCD

Lt Col Phillip Boroff, 498MUMG/CD

Lt Col Earl Bennett, AF/A8PC

Lt Col Tony Crews, USAF CMD/DS/J1

Lt Col Scott Diezman, SAF/USA

Lt Col Eric Johnson, AF/A1PF

Lt Col John Moes, AF/A7SO

Lt Col Joseph Newberry, NGB/A4M

Lt Col Lenny Richoux, SAF/CMX

Maj John DeVincenzo, AF/SEI

Maj Walter Jackim, AF/A5XP

Maj Thad Middleton, AF/A9R

Maj David Slye, SAF/IGI

Maj Kendal Stevenson, AF/A3O-ST

Capt Elizabeth Aptekar, SAF/PAD

Ms. Jacqueline Clark, SAF/CMX

Mr. Robert Tilson, AF/A3/5N-O

Mr. James Vaz, AF/A3/5N-P

Additional Team Members

Col Charles Armentrout, AF/A1PP

Col James Dunn, ACC/CV-N

Col Sandra Finan, AFSPC/CVN

Col Mohammed Khan, AF/A8PS

Lt Col Lance Adkins, AFSPC/A8XN

Lt Col Robert Drozd, AF/A5XP

Lt Col Juan Gacharna, AFSO21

Lt Col John Sweeney, ACC/A3SD

Maj Jason Knudson, AF/A7SO

Maj William Lynch, AF/A8PC

Capt Brian Stone, AF/A9AO

Capt Yuri Taitano, AF/A9AO

Mr. James Crum, AF/A3/5N-O

Dr. Mark Gallagher, AF/A9R

Ms. Julie George, SAF/CMX

Mr. Stephen Key, HAF/IMEP

Mr. Benny Martin, AFSC/SEWN

Mr. Darphaus Mitchell, AF/A3/5N-O

Task Force Support

Col George Farfour, AF/A3/5N-O

Col Timothy Ferguson, ACC/A7S-2

Col Donald Flowers, AFIA/CV

Col Michael Morris, AFPC/DPAP

Lt Col James Baxter; AF/A9LG

Lt Col Laura Berry, SAF/CMX

Lt Col Reyes Colon, AF/A5RS

Lt Col David Fewster, AFSPC/CVO

Lt Col Rodney Hart, AFSPC/A8XN

Lt Col Joseph Heilhecker, SAF/SO

Lt Col Matthew Keihl, AFIA/EL

Lt Col David Miller, AF/A3O-I

Lt Col Clark Risner, AF/A3O-SO

Maj Paul Cazier, AETC/A3TB

Maj Veronica Hutfles, ACC/CCX

Maj Michael Miller, AF/A3O-AT

CMSgt Lorne Larson, USAFE/A3NM

SMSgt Jeffrey Haakinson, AFSPC/A7SON

SMSgt John Mister, AFSPC/A4MI

MSgt Miguel Garza, AFSC/SEWN

MSgt Shawn Joy, AMC/A3NA

MSgt John Oblinger, AF/A7S

Dr. David Carter, AF/A3/5N

Dr. Todd Fore, AF/A1D

Dr. Suzanne Logan, AETC AWC/CD

Mr. Larry Akin, ACC/CV-N

Mr. John Howard, AETC/MXDB

Mr. Thomas Noon, AF/A4R-1

A54

Integrity-Service-Excellence

A Roadmap to Reinvigorate the Air Force Nuclear Enterprise

www.ingramcontent.com/pod-product-compliance
Lightning Source LLC
Chambersburg PA
CBHW080255290526
45790CB00005B/1824